PENGUIN BOOKS

NOT TONIGHT, MR RIGHT

Kate Taylor is the published author of three sex books and was the high-profile writer of *GQ*'s 'Sex life' column from 1998 to 2002 (when it was voted 'Best page in *GQ*' every year by readers). She has also written for many other publications, including the *Guardian*, the *Observer*, *Minx*, *She*, *More!*, the *Sun* and *Tatler*. Kate presented *Sex Tips for Girls* (2001) on Channel 4, is the expert on Match.com, and has been hailed as 'Britain's Candace Bushnell' by those who should know. She is married and lives in Surrey. She didn't sleep with her husband for an eternity after they met, and he's still complaining about it – and still buying her flowers.

Not Tonight, Mr Right

Why good men come to girls who wait

KATE TAYLOR

PENGUIN BOOKS

PENGUIN BOOKS

Published by the Penguin Group
Penguin Books Ltd, 80 Strand, London WC2R ORL, England
Penguin Group (USA) Inc., 375 Hudson Street, New York, New York 10014, USA
Penguin Group (Canada), 90 Eglinton Avenue East, Suite 700, Toronto, Ontario, Canada M4P 2Y3
(a division of Pearson Penguin Canada Inc.)
Penguin Ireland, 25 St Stephen's Green, Dublin 2, Ireland (a division of Penguin Books Ltd)
Penguin Group (Australia), 250 Camberwell Road, Camberwell, Victoria 3124, Australia
(a division of Pearson Australia Group Pty Ltd)
Penguin Books India Pvt Ltd, 11 Community Centre, Panchsheel Park, New Delhi – 110 017, India
Penguin Group (NZ), 67 Apollo Drive, Mairangi Bay, Auckland 1310, New Zealand
(a division of Pearson New Zealand Ltd)
Penguin Books (South Africa) (Pty) Ltd, 24 Sturdee Avenue,
Rosebank, Johannesburg 2196, South Africa

Penguin Books Ltd, Registered Offices: 80 Strand, London WC2R ORL, England

www.penguin.com

First published 2007
1

Every effort has been made to trace copyright holders and we
apologize in advance for any unintentional omission. We would
be pleased to insert the appropriate acknowledgement in
any subsequent edition.

Set in 11.5/16.5 pt Adobe Garamond
Typeset by Rowland Phototypesetting Ltd, Bury St Edmunds, Suffolk
Printed in England by Clays Ltd, St Ives plc

ISBN: 978-0-141-01927-7

To Valerie Savage, who knew
a thing or two about men.

'There are three possible parts to a date, of which at least two must be offered: entertainment, food and affection. It is customary to begin a series of dates with a great deal of entertainment, a moderate amount of food and the mere suggestion of affection. As the amount of affection increases, the entertainment can be reduced proportionally. When the affection is the entertainment, we no longer call it dating.'

Miss Manners

Contents

Introduction

Keep your knickers on. Change your life.

Wendy Keller

'To make a man fall in love with you, give him the best sex he's ever had, or no sex at all.' That piece of wisdom was passed on to me by a work colleague when I was eighteen. Up until then I'd been following the second part of it perfectly. I still hadn't had sex, and wouldn't for another year, when I got engaged.

It made a lot of sense to me. I'd always known that men went nuts when you denied them nookie. At that age, I still wasn't too interested in getting involved with my boyfriends so I was perfectly calm about slamming the front door on their erections after a date. They kept phoning me, they kept seeing me. They might have moaned occasionally, but I just reminded them that there were billions of women in the world to have sex with, and if that's all they wanted, they could leave.

They never left.

I was always very cool about these boyfriends and couldn't understand why my friends were getting so keen on theirs (whom they were shagging). I had girlfriends who'd call me up at midnight in tears, because their boyfriend had been seen out with someone else. 'Well, chuck him then,' I'd say, nonplussed. 'It's not that simple!' they'd sob. 'I love him.'

'But you have to love yourself first,' I'd explain, patiently. 'He doesn't sound like he's being very nice to you.' At which point they'd hang up on me and go find someone more understanding to talk to.

I got engaged to a sweet man when I was nineteen, and lost my virginity. It was quite disappointing, though, so I quickly found it again, and broke off the engagement. But then at university I decided I was a feminist and could therefore go out and use men for sex any time I liked.

That was the point I became the world's worst dater. Over the next few years I made every mistake you can make with a boyfriend. I chased them, I said 'I love you' first. I made one a PUPPET OF HIMSELF for Valentine's Day and couldn't understand why his friends thought I was a nutcase. I thought it was 'sweet' when a man turned up at my flat at 2am wanting sex. I convinced myself that jewellery was something women bought for themselves, and dinner dates meant never having to say, 'Thanks for paying.'

Then, as you'd expect, at twenty-seven I finally had my heart sat on like a pair of sunglasses and spent a year moping at home, refusing to see anyone except for Ben & Jerry. During those months I found an old diary I'd kept at seventeen. As I opened it, a poem fell out that a boyfriend had written me. I read entry after entry about sweet dates I'd been taken on, nice things they'd said to me, proposals I'd been given. And all of it written in the most down-to-earth, calm voice. I barely recognized myself. So I decided I'd go back to my seventeen-year-old self and start keeping my feet on the ground instead of hooking them round a man's neck.

Yes, it was often hard. It was often very hard. It was often very hard and pressed up against my leg as I kissed my boyfriend goodnight, but I *still* didn't have sex. And at this point, I was a sex columnist for *GQ* magazine and the author of a best-selling sex manual, *The Good Orgasm Guide*. My entire career was about nookie, I could put condoms through as business expenses. All my best girlfriends were sex columnists and writers. So it was a radical move to start re-fusing sex. However, having a team of writers as friends was a big help, because all of us agreed that withholding sex was a vastly under-used dating tactic. Even though all of us wrote sex tips and advice for a living, privately we swapped tips on how not to give up the goods. Knowing men's sexual prefer-ences so well, we knew that men find women more intriguing when they have the confidence to keep their knees together.

Did it work? Yes. Within two years, I'd met the man I wanted and got engaged to him, and this time everything was lovely and we got married.

So. What follows, in this book, is my guide to being the girl who *can* say No. Everything here is written either from my own tortuous personal experience, or learned in the six years I wrote *GQ*'s Sex Column and interviewed thousands of men, and received letters from many others. It was also helped greatly by the many women who agreed to be interviewed about their own experiences with waiting to have sex.

In here you'll find everything you need to follow a simple plan of 'tactical abstinence' until you've found your own Mr Right. Why to say No, how to say No, when to say No, who to say No to, and finally, happily, ecstatically, when to say, 'Oh God yes, please, now, YES!'

With love,

Kate

www.nottonightmrright.com

Quiz

How Much Do You Need This Book?

1. Have you ever had sex when, looking back, a simple 'Thanks for dinner' or 'I'm sorry I forgot your birthday' would have sufficed?

2. Have you ever tried to win back a bored boyfriend with a complicated technique called something like, 'Crouching Tiger, Hidden Hard-On'?

3. Have you ever got naked just to relieve outside pressure – from your friends, your man, or your control-top underwear?

4. Have you ever had sex with someone you weren't that keen on, but still felt irrationally annoyed when they didn't call you again afterwards? Or worse, felt irrationally relieved when they did?

5. Have you ever wished you knew the perfect moment to bonk?

Answers:

Count the number of times you've said Yes. Not to men (we don't have all day), just to the questions.

- 1–5: Run, don't walk, to the till and buy this book

immediately. Try not to have sex with anyone on the way.

- **0:** You are naturally a Lofty Love Goddess. Put this book down and go and buy something about weddings.

1

The Thrill of the Chaste

*I like the way guys go crazy when they can't have sex with
you. If he can't have you, he stays interested. The moment he
has you, he's gone, unless he is really in love with you.*

Paris Hilton

In this book, I'm going to show you how to establish the
easiest, most secure and longest-lasting relationships you've
ever had. Relationships that are fun, blissfully content and
happy, and fill you with a sense of peace. Relationships that
are the envy of your friends, and the agony of your exes.
And to achieve relationships like these, you don't have to play
any games, count your boyfriend's phone calls, or agonize
over how he's treating you. All you have to do is not have
sex with him.

'*What?*'

Hmm? Why are you staring at this page in horror? Oh . . .
you noticed the bit about not having sex, did you? I sort of

hoped I could just slip that in there casually without you noticing – something men have been trying to do for years. But, yes. That's the point of the book. To show you how you can upgrade your dating, simply by not leaping into bed until you've reached a level of commitment you're happy with *first*. As we'll see in a minute, the time limit will differ for everyone, but certainly you shouldn't be planning on touching anything hairy for the first six months. It doesn't have to be six months to the day – I haven't devised some cunning marketing ploy where I'm going to sell little half-year Nookie Planners – but you should be waiting until you know exactly where the relationship is going.

I know what you're thinking now: 'But I know where the relationship will be going – nowhere! Who in their right mind will date me for six months without getting any action?' The answer is: anyone who adores you. Men who love you will wait, happily, until *you* are ready for sex. Men don't expect to have sex on the first, third or fiftieth date. They don't have an expiry date on their penis, it doesn't come with a 'Best Before' sticker. If they love you, they will wait until you're ready. And the ones who don't will get bored and wander off. Which is a *good* thing.

Yes, I know that doesn't sound like a good thing. I don't blame you if you're not leaping up and down in excitement at the thought of being chucked by the next promising new man you meet. The fact is that nobody relishes a chucking. But you will be staggered by the number of men who will *not* dump you for keeping your knickers on. If you don't believe me, skip ahead to Chapter Seven where men are waiting to tell you honestly what they think about Women Who Wait. It's not 'frigid wastes of time', it's 'smart girls with standards'.

Now, I know I'm not the first person to have given you this advice. If your Mum hasn't tried to drum it into you, your Dad will have. I'd even guess that you've always instinctively known that waiting to have sex was a good idea. But there's a difference between knowing not to have sex early on, and knowing how to follow that advice. That's what I'm really hoping you'll get from this book – a solid, helpful template on how to have sex-free relationships without losing your marbles or your man.

When people breezily advise, 'Oh, just make him wait for a bit,' they never seem to realize how terrifying that can be, especially when you're dating someone you think might be The One. While you sit there with your thoughts spinning like a tumble drier – 'How long is "a bit"? Should I tell him up front? Do I get T-shirts printed? Or underwear? Can I go to third base with him – is that too much? Will he think I'm a bit Christian? Will he chuck me? Will he bonk someone else in the meantime? Argh!' – your helpful adviser disappears to get on with their day and you're left in agony. It just seems so complicated, especially today when the same magazines that offer the 'Wait for it!' advice columns have covers festooned with lines like, 'Give him the Best Sex Ever' and 'Fifty Things To Do With a Jar of Marmite That He'll Have Never Felt Before'.

So I don't blame you if you end up horizontal because it all just seems a lot easier.

But be assured – it's not easier. One thing people never explain when they proffer that age-old 'Keep your knickers on' advice is that dating without sex is calmer, more peaceful, and a million times less stressful than dating *with* sex. The reason is oxytocin.

Oxytocin – the Fatal Attraction Hormone

Many things go on inside your body when you start making love. From the first passionate kisses, your heart-rate rises, blood rushes to your nether regions and your pituitary gland starts releasing a hormone called oxytocin. Its job is to help you orgasm (*note to body: maybe putting the clitoris somewhere actually* near *the vagina might have done that more efficiently*), and to increase the feelings of attachment you have towards your partner.

Oxytocin is the Love Juice that makes you not mind when your partner rams his elbow in your eye-socket and kneels on your windpipe. It's what makes you want to cuddle him for ages after sex. It's what makes you overlook little annoying habits of his – like being male – and it's what makes love so blind and *binding*.

The effects of oxytocin don't wear off immediately after sex because the hormone can stay in your body for two years. Yes, two years. Count them. Because oxytocin is also released during childbirth, scientists believe it hangs around for so long to help the mother not go, basically, 'Oh sod this,' and throw her offspring over a cliff in their first years of life. Which is fine when you're talking about a *baby*. But not half as fine when you're talking about the other useless lump that lies around the house burping all day: that man you just bonked.

Every time you have sex with a man you are risking forming an incredibly intense attachment to him. Unlike you, oxytocin doesn't try to weigh up a man's character values or check if his flowers came from a garage before it begins the bonding process. Instead, it just hurls itself into your bloodstream the minute he starts tweaking your nipples and giving you orgasms. Ever fallen for a typical Bad Boy because the sex was incredible? This is why. The more orgasms you receive, the stronger the ties that bind you.

When you're experiencing oxytocin bonding, you're literally addicted to the man who set it off. His voice on your answerphone, his hand on your shoulder, even his smell can jumpstart your heart-rate and the brain chemicals responsible for your happiness, trust and intuition. Suddenly everything he does or says is vitally important to you. If you've ever shown a man's text message to 150 of your friends, asking, 'But what does he *mean* by "Hello"?' you've experienced oxytocin. If you've ever justified his sleeping with someone else, or ignored everyone who advised you that maybe, just maybe, his emigrating to Australia wasn't *that* good a sign, you've felt it at its worst. Oxytocin is the hormone that can make you go psychotic with infatuation, and unable to shake off your obsession with a man. Maybe that's why they call it 'going bonkers'.

To break its bonds, you have to go cold-turkey. There's no gradual weaning-off. You have to have no contact with the man for at least two months, but preferably up to a year. Even hearing his voice on the telephone, or wearing his old T-shirt to bed, can keep you hooked.

But there's an even crueller trick that Mother Nature has played on us. Whilst men release oxytocin (and another bonding-chemical called vasopressin) during sex, their effects can be completely neutralized by testosterone. So the more testosterone a man has in his system, potentially the less likely he is to bond to you after nookage. And who is most likely to give you long nights of bed-breaking bonking? A man *filled to the brim* with testosterone, because he'll be stronger, fitter, and have a higher libido.

Gulp.

A man doesn't have the same amount of testosterone inside his body for all of his life. Research has shown that a man's testosterone levels will drop when he gets married, and drop further still when he has children. But it will rise if he starts arguing with his wife, and rise again if he gets divorced. But when is it usually at its all-time peak? When he's single.

So, to summarize: every time you get into bed with a man

to whom you're not married, you're risking kicking off a bonding process that will make you crazy in love for the next two years. You're more at risk if he's any good between the sheets. And you're *especially* at risk if he's single.

Right then! Who's up for a rogering?

Smart Girls Don't

If you feel that withholding sex from a man to encourage him to fall in love with you is manipulation, you're absolutely right. But if you think that makes it a bad thing to do, you're absolutely wrong. Not satisfying a man's sexual desire for you is the very best way to encourage his initial feelings of lust to turn into something far stronger – love.

When a man first meets you, he is not immediately stricken with the desire to have a long-term relationship with you. He doesn't spot you across a crowded room and think, 'Her in the red dress – that is the woman I must have to clean behind my refrigerator.' He isn't shot with an urge to take you to Sainsbury's to do a big food-shop. What he wants to do is put his choo-choo into your tunnel.

In the old days, of course, to get that pleasure he had to marry you, which is where all our courtship rituals come from. Dinner for two was born because a man was trying to demonstrate his ability to *provide*. He was saying, 'Marry me and I can put food on your table.' The presents were saying, 'Marry me and I can give you the things which please you.' And the dresses and jewellery were saying, 'I am a man of status and, if you marry me, you will be looked upon with envy.'

And what did he get in return for marrying you? A darned good seeing-to. And better, he stopped other men from having the pleasure of your company.

This is the way it works in the animal kingdom too. The Sexual Revolution hasn't hit the insect world, and so the females of most species can still only be wooed and won with little gifts of food. Some use this to their advantage – for example, the female Mormon cricket won't mate with a male until he has brought her something to eat. They have sex whilst she is eating the food – craftily encouraging him to bring her loads of the stuff, because as soon as the food runs out, so does the shag. (Don't try this at an 'all you can eat' buffet, by the way.)

The females of our species are now officially the least choosy on the planet, which is just downright embarrassing. Even tiny midges are tougher than us. The female midge will eat her partner while he is bonking her, so she gets bed and breakfast. What do we get? A ready meal and a thrilling evening watching *Match of the Day* re-runs.

What makes us less choosy? One of the main reasons has to be contraception. Because we're now in charge of deciding whether or not we get pregnant, we don't have to put our men through an intensive wining-and-dining screening process. Which has made our standards – and our knickers – drop rapidly. It's understandable that women would go sex-mad as soon as we could control our fertility, and of course it's brilliant that you don't have to risk raising the gormless child of every man you ever regretted waking up next to. But just because you *can* have immediate sex with anyone you like doesn't mean you *should*.

If you sleep with a man right away, you are throwing away your best chance of making him become absolutely wild about you. A survey of 200 daters, conducted by American psychologists Martie Haselton and Dr David Buss in 2001, revealed conclusively that men found their partners *less* attractive and sexy after first-time sex than they did before. And the more partners a man had had, the more likely he was to think his lover was a minger in the morning.

Women, in contrast, always found their partners *more* sexy after that first bonk, regardless of their number of previous partners.

So, unsurprisingly, people have been advising women for-ever to wait. Here's the Roman poet Ovid trying to encourage women in 50BC to keep their togas on:

Now if too soon you yield, too soon you'll lose your love. Denials must be sometimes mingled with dalliance. You must sometimes keep your lover begging and praying and threatening before your door. Sweet things are bad for us. Bitters are the best tonic for the jaded appetite.

Doris Langley-Moore wrote a book in the 1920s called *The Technique of the Love Affair*, which advised women how to capture the few remaining men that made it home after World War I. In those days women were experiencing more independence, and Flappers were starting to veer towards becoming Slappers. Langley-Moore tried to discourage them:

It is not advisable ... to take [sexual] experience with the man with whom you wish to marry, until your mating has been duly sanctioned and solemnized – not because he will necessarily respect you less afterwards, but simply because he will desire you less and will therefore feel less inducement to bind himself to you ... Even if in the test of possession he finds that you satisfy his most extravagant ideals, still his curiosity for physical knowledge of you will be appeased, and that forms no inconsiderable portion of desire.

And 'Love easily obtained is of little value; difficulty in obtaining it makes it precious' was the twelfth-century version of *The Rules*, by poet Andreas Capellanus.

When texts like these were written, the authors didn't know *why* abstinence was tactically a good idea; just that it worked. Today, however, we know the reason. Dopamine.

Complicated Science Bit

When we are initially attracted to someone, dopamine is released in the brain. This is just one of several chemicals that come out during the attraction process – the brains of people in love look like the inside of Pete Doherty's flat – but it's the one we're most interested in here because it stimulates the hypothalamus region of the brain. As one anonymous psychology professor explained it:

The hypothalamus is one of the most important parts of the brain, involved in many kinds of motivation, among other functions. It controls the 'Four Fs': fighting, fleeing, feeding and mating.

Scientists have found that early acquisition of a reward reduces the intensity and duration of dopamine activity in the brain. But a delayed reward increases it. So, the longer you make a man wait before he achieves his reward, the more excited and happy he'll be.

But there's more to it than that – dopamine has been associated with intense motivation. Anthropologist Dr Helen Fisher conducted brain scans on people who admitted they were 'madly in love' and found that, when they were encouraged to think about their beloved, they all showed striking activity in the ventral tegmental area of the brain, which sends dopamine to many other parts of the brain. When stimulated, this area produces focussed attention, fierce energy, concentrated motivation and feelings akin to mania. As Fisher writes in *Why We Love*:

No wonder lovers talk all night or walk till dawn, write extravagant poetry, cross continents or oceans just for a hug.

The upshot of all of this is, the longer you make a man wait to receive his reward (you), the more motivated he will be to spend time with you, and the longer that motivation will last.

And it is at this peak of your partner's motivation that you should be laying down your terms before you lay down on your mattress. Think of sex as a negotiation. Your man's impulse is to ravish you. What do you want in return?

How Long to Wait Before Sex

How long you wait depends purely on what you're looking for. But you should know what you want *before* you bonk.

Love?

You might just want to wait until you're 100 per cent sure of your partner's affection for you. This is the least I'd recommend. There's nothing more miserable than getting bonded to a man who sees you as a 'good for now' girl but has no long-term plans in mind. The safest time is six months into the relationship. This gets you past the tricky three-month period when most men start to evaluate whether they want a long-term partner or just a stand-in. If you look back over your relationships you'll see that lots of them ended around the twelve-week time. It's like pregnancy – often it takes twelve weeks for a relationship to implant. In fact, it's wise not to announce pregnancies *or* boyfriends until the first three months have passed. For those of you in your twenties who aren't looking to go wedding-dress shopping any time soon, this is probably the best choice for you. And equally, it's a good choice as you get older. After the menopause your testosterone levels will rise, so you're less likely to get heavily bonded by oxytocin. Casual sex is safer for you. Plus, men over forty start losing testosterone so are more likely to become naturally committed anyway.

Engagement?

You might prefer to wait until you are even more sure of his affections. In this case, engagement is a good time. It's not as daunting as waiting until your wedding night, but equally, it's not as safe if marriage is the *only* thing you'll settle for. If you're in your late twenties or early thirties I'd say wait until engagement. If nothing else it means you can bonk your heart out to relieve the stress of planning the wedding.

Marriage?

This will probably be your choice if you're religious, but it could also be your choice if you're in your mid- to late-thirties and are keen to start a family. When you wait until your wedding night you're guarding your heart the most. At that point you know your man is committed to you, and sex goes back to its traditional role as a celebration of the union between a man and his wife. It also gives a bigger finale to the wedding night rather than just walking under a balloon archway.

Note: All these choices sound daunting when you're used to having sex as you date. When sex is involved, men take longer to commit, so engagements and marriages usually happen after two or three years. But when you abstain from casual sex, everything happens a LOT quicker. You could easily be engaged after six months and married within the year. Abstinence makes his heart grow fonder, and much more decisive.

All the Fun of the Affair

If your thoughts are currently churning, occasionally throwing out the odd sentence like, 'But sex is often the only good bit of a bad date,' and, 'Bonking is the only part of dating I know how to do,' this is the section for you. Waiting before you have sex with someone new doesn't mean waiting before you have fun. In many ways, you're going to enjoy yourself *more* by remaining vertical.

How come? Because you get to focus on the really nice bits about dating – when your boyfriend is genuinely in love with you. Let's be honest here, after a really good date, what parts are you most proud to boast about with your girlfriends? It's *not* the nookie – you don't see a cluster of females standing round sighing and looking wistful when one of them is re-telling the part about getting her fringe caught in his flies. You see them standing round, shiny-eyed and jealous, when one of them is describing the billboard poster her boyfriend had done with a proposal on it, or the enormous bouquet of imported flowers he sent over, or that he stayed awake through *Sleepless in Seattle* and didn't complain.

We instinctively love hearing this stuff because it's roman-tic, and romance is what happens when a man genuinely cares about you. And a man who genuinely cares is much more likely to stick around and help raise any offspring. So you're not being a princess if you want a man who treats you well, you are being a woman.

Most women are cynical about romance these days, think-ing that, if it's not dead, then it certainly has a nasty cough that ought to be looked at. And I think we're more cynical now than we ever have been, because equality makes it easy to be a lazy boyfriend and get away with it. Suddenly, refusing to pay for dinner isn't 'stingy', it's 'allowing the woman to make an equal contribution to the relationship'. Living together isn't 'making sure I don't meet someone better', it's 'a way to take our love to the next level without big risks for both of us'. All of the most disappointing parts of modern dating sound okay because you can spin them in your head so they don't sound bleak and loveless. You can counter your disappointment that he still hasn't proposed by saying, 'Well, I'm not sure if I'm ready for marriage either, so it's good we're taking it slowly,' rather than face up to it honestly and rage, 'The twat! It's been twenty-seven years!'

Relationship books make us feel bad because they try to talk us out of analyzing dating. They say things like, 'Don't set up an abacus on your phone table to count how many times he rings you. Just focus on your own life, go and have fun!' which is good, of course, but it ignores the fact that we *always* analyze when we date. We do it instinctively, because we need to ensure we get a good, devoted, dependable dad for our children. Psychologists call this 'parental investment'. The person who has the biggest investment in raising a child – the woman – is likely to be the most choosy about selecting their mate. Remember, you might know that you've put your biological clock on snooze, but your ovaries don't. Your body is still set up to get pregnant if you have sex.

When we have sex, that analytical urge is dampened by the oxytocin. One of the effects of this hormone is to boost feelings of trust between lovers. This isn't the same as Lust Goggles, when you feel shallow for liking someone just because you find them sexy so you try to attach other qualities, like kindness and intelligence, to them. The oxytocin effect makes you give your partner the benefit of the doubt. It helps silence that nagging voice which is saying to you, 'Er, but if he really liked you, wouldn't he have called?'

Of course, trust is a necessary part of a committed relationship, but *not* in the early stages. The beginning of dating is the time for you to watch your man's actions and assess his character and see if he's good enough for you. When you have sex on the first few dates, often you merely start to worry if *you're* good enough for *him*.

Unless you're a testosterone-fuelled ball-breaker, you'll feel happier when you are being actively pursued by your partner. What's happening today is that the dream of 'equality in love' is encouraging us to take on fifty per cent of the pursuing because, *ideally*, that would work really well. In a perfect world, of course we'd be able to ask men out, call them a lot, and be the one to drop to one knee with a ring. So we do these things, hoping that we're getting one step closer to Paradise.

Are we? I don't think so. Be honest: what happens when you have first-night nookie with a man you *really* like? Do you wake up feeling relaxed and secure? Sometimes. Now, fast-forward to five days later when he still hasn't got in touch. How do you feel then? Serene and blissful? Or sickened and gutted? That's about the time that you arrange a Crisis Meeting with your girlfriends and get drunk in the bar, raging that 'all men are rubbish'.

But all men *aren't* rubbish. Putting yourself in a vulnerable position is rubbish. Following bad dating advice is rubbish. Not believing you're worthy of being courted is rubbish. And believing women can have sex as light-and-breezily as men is rubbish too.

For one thing, men like to have higher numbers of sexual partners than women. Research by Dr David Buss, an American psychologist, showed that the average number of sexual partners women would like to have in their lifetime is 4.5. Men would like **eighteen**. And for another, women are much pickier than men when choosing partners for even *casual* sex.

A behavioural study conducted in America (Clarke & Hatfield, 1989) confirmed this difference. Male and female researchers were sent to a university campus to chat up members of the opposite sex. After some brief flattery – 'Hi, I've noticed you around for a while now and I find you very attractive' – the researchers were told to ask one of three questions and make a note of the respondents' answers and comments.

The questions were:

1. Would you go on a date with me?
2. Would you come back to my place with me?
3. Would you have sex with me?

Of the women approached by the male experimenters, fifty per cent agreed to a date; six per cent agreed to go back to his place; and none agreed to a bunk-up. But the men, well, you can guess. Fifty per cent agreed to go out on a date; sixty-nine per cent agreed to go back to her place. And **seventy-five** per cent agreed to nookie.

If women were designed to have casual sex as easily as men, we'd jump at the chance of a jump. Of course, you could assume that women are unlikely to have sex with a stranger who approaches them because of the danger of being attacked. But that doesn't explain the other research (cited by Dr Fisher) which shows that when women are searching for a casual-sex partner, they look for the following qualities: he must be healthy, stable, funny, kind and generous.

Now that makes no sense. Surely, for a quick, no-strings shag, the only legitimate criterion is 'willy like a marrow'. If you'd had some bad experiences you could add other must-haves like 'not allergic to soap', or 'doesn't insist on using proper Police handcuffs'. But funny? Generous? That's not a perfect shag, it's a perfect mate.

All of this explains why we feel unstable when we go bed-hopping. We're not designed to do it. And that explains why women feel calmer, happier and more secure in a relationship that is committed and secure *before* they get under the duvet.

I'll now take some questions from the floor

There is no way in holy hell I would wait until marriage. Or even engagement. With my luck, I'll get landed with the world's worst lover for a husband.

No you won't. Believe me, you'll know if a man is any good in bed without actually pushing him down on the carpet for a test-drive. Just his kissing technique, for example, will tell you a lot: how experienced he is (does he nervously lean in for a kiss, or confidently pin you up against your front door?); how much foreplay he's into (a man disinterested in foreplay will try to skip past the kissing stage and get straight to work on your blouse buttons); and how much chemistry you have together (whether his kisses make you feel 'Ooh!' or 'Eww!'). There isn't that much magic in just the thrusty stage of sex. Think back: the men who drove you wild with passion were making you feel excited HOURS before they actually started humping you.

That's all I'm trying to get you to do – find a man who excites and thrills you *before* he wears out your mattress cover.

Listen, sorry to be so frank and everything, but if I'm not, um, 'checking out the merchandise' before I get involved in a relationship, surely I could easily get saddled with an – oh help, this is embarrassing – under-endowed man?

I don't advocate waiting until marriage to see how big his bits are. I mean, I don't advocate demanding to know on the first date either, turning up with a magnifying glass and a ruler, but there are ways of establishing his size without actually inserting him. I've found the size of a man's feet to be pretty reliable. If he's still wearing kiddies' training shoes at the age of thirty, I think you can rest assured that he's not packing much more than a baby prawn down his boxers.

But why are we even talking about this? If you think that girth is the secret to long-lasting relationships, you're wrong. How about you spend those early dates checking out the size of the other vital bits of him? His brain, for example. His generosity. His sense of humour. How long he stays with you just because he loves being with you, not because you're merrily 'sampling his wares' on the third date.

How would you feel if a man ditched you because he found out that you were sporting chicken fillets in your bra? I know you secretly think you'd be quite modern and grown-up about it, but deep down you'd feel he was shallower than a saucer. And you'd be right.

I've slept with loads of men before, and never bonded with any of them. In fact, most of them ended up getting keen on me while I remained not bothered about them! I think you're talking rubbish.

Ahhh, but that just proves my point. By 'sleeping with loads of men', you've shown that you are a woman with high levels of testosterone. Women with higher levels will be more sexually aggressive than the other, more kittens-and-white-chocolate type of girls. You're a lot more likely to pursue sex, and less likely to be as emotionally affected. You'll also be more aggressive in the workplace, if you're not just using your desk to bonk on. However, this doesn't give you a licence to romp. Most women's baseline of oxytocin is still up to ten times higher than the average man's, so you will still find yourself more affected than your partner. Which is fine if you want to carry on having meaningless nookie, but what about when you meet someone with whom you want to settle down?

♥

I'm not the type to go for long periods without some stimulation. How will I satisfy my needs for six months?

We'll get to that in Chapter Two. I suggest you skip to that bit straight away.

♥

This sounds to me like playing games.

It's not playing games, it's using a strategy. There's a difference. Playing games is when you pretend to be someone other than yourself – when you let the phone ring on Saturday nights because you want to be seen as popular, rather than agoraphobic and addicted to online Sudoku. Using a strategy means you gather all the knowledge you can about a topic – in this case, men – and use that information to influence your behaviour.

♥

You said 'women have been doing this for centuries' like it's a good thing. I'd have thought that it was time for some new ways to date. Should we also give up the Vote and go back to the kitchen?

I knew this was coming. To quote Langley-Moore again:

… even today it might be regarded a little destructive to feminine charm to announce an individual claim [to sexual experience] and it is the charm, not the emancipation of our sex, which is the subject of this work.

I'm not arguing about whether it is *right* that men can go off us after sex, just that it is possible or even probable. Yes, it's a bummer, but what are you going to do? We can't rewire men's brains. We can't inoculate ourselves against oxytocin. All we can do is work with things as they stand. And not lie down too fast.

Okay, fair enough. But I'm not looking for commitment, just a boyfriend. Why six months? That seems a bit extreme. I usually wait about six weeks. Or six dates.

That's not bad. I've known women who only wait six *drinks*. The reason I've set the timer for six months is that's usually how long it takes for you to know if he's a safe bet. Men fall in love quicker than women, but they also fall out of love quicker, so six months is about right to make sure he's not suddenly going to start talking about 'fear of commitment' and 'needing time to get my head straight'. It's also long enough to weed out the most persevering of players.

You said you were going to go into this subject deeply, but I still don't know how to date without sex. Like, when do I tell him? Should I ban him from sleepovers? Should I get a vibrator? Should I . . .?

All that and more is coming up next, in Chapter Two.

2

And So Not to Bed

Women might be able to fake orgasms. But men can fake whole relationships.

Sharon Stone

You've probably always assumed it was pretty easy not to have sex. Surely, you'd think, you just get up in the morning and go through your day normally. It's not as if most of our days are spent beating men back with umbrellas on the bus, or pushing through a row of erections to buy a sandwich. How hard can it be not to have any nookie on the average night? Married people do it for years.

Ah yes, but that's because you weren't trying not to have sex. It's like dieting. One minute you are going about your business, eating whatever you fancy, and generally not thinking too much about food. Then you go on a diet. From that moment onwards, you're obsessed. Your first thought in the morning is what you can have for breakfast. Your last thought at night is what you're going to have for breakfast. Suddenly you're being charged with stalking because you keep following people on the street who are eating Snickers bars . . .

So, the first thing to be prepared for as you embark on this new way of dating is that you'll probably immediately notice an increase in your sex-drive. From being the sort of girl who thinks about sex a few times a week, or just that day right before your period, your brain begins to resemble that of a life-sentence prison inmate. You'll start driving out of your way just to hit a few speed-bumps, and you'll find yourself groaning in an embarrassing, involuntary way, watching love scenes in Corrie.

Or, you'll just find yourself in a slight stage of arousal for a while. This is only because sex has now become the Forbidden Fruit. That's a *good* thing. Already you are starting to view sex as something special and powerful and precious – rather than simply a way to while away the time till the kettle boils.

But before you worry that you'll be caught humping a loo brush in the office lavatories, I can tell you that this stage will not last very long. Depending on factors like your age (women's sex drives increase as they get older), where you are in your menstrual cycle (we are more likely to become aroused between around day twelve and day twenty-seven), and whether or not you were a virgin (it's obviously easier to miss sex when you've *had* sex), this 'I'm horny – horny, horny, horny' stage lasts for about two or three weeks. Some of you might not notice it at all.

It'll be strongest if, prior to taking a Keep Your Knickers On vow, you were either a: in a long-term relationship where you had regular sex; or b: putting yourself about a bit. When you have regular sex over a long period of time, your body gets used to it and your sex drive will remain higher than that of a singleton. The more you have sex, the more you want it. Unless you're having it with my ex.

However, as soon as sex has become something rare and prized, you'll find yourself thinking about it less frequently.

I wanted to address this libido rise, because it can really knock your resolve. It's easy to convince yourself that craving sex is a sign from On High that you shouldn't give it up. It's not. It's a sign from Down Below that you've missed the normal Friday-night rush. Remember, you're just breaking a habit. This isn't forever. So, put that cucumber down and we'll talk about ways to make the transition from Goer to No-Goer a lot easier.

How Not to Have Sex – When You're Single

If you're reading this book when there is nobody in your life you'd even shag blind-folded, you're lucky. I know it doesn't feel that way, but you are. You have plenty of time to adjust to your new mindset before you meet anyone tempting, so you can absorb all the following tips which should help boost your resolve. Later on, we'll talk about how to date without doing it.

Break Your Rampant-Rabbit Habit

Do you have vibrators lurking in your bedside cabinet? Of course you don't. And neither do I. (Cough.) But if you did, I'd advise you to put them away for the time being. The reason is, you want your libido to calm down. Every time you orgasm, whether it's through bonking your boyfriend or wearing down the batteries in your vibrator, you're keeping your sex drive at a high rev. Just avoiding any kind of sexual stimulation at ALL for a couple of weeks will dull your urges. (This sounds a lot harder than it actually is, by the way.)

If you're someone who likes to masturbate to relax, or to get off to sleep, take a few supplements for the first month. Things like Valerian Root and Vitamin B Complex can calm you down.

Break Your Addiction to Nookie

Breaking any kind of long-term habit causes us to go through a period of loss, especially if (like sex) it was a habit that boosted the reward pathways in our brain. Even people who give up smoking notice this. No matter how well-intentioned they are, the stages of breaking the addiction are the same. You might sail through the first week or two of not having sex but if you don't, consciously working through the five stages of Grief – the universal stages of loss, identified by

Elisabeth Kübler-Ross – might help. You'll be going through them anyway, so it's good to know what's coming.

Stage One: Denial

Until you're completely behind the idea of waiting a while before you have sex, you might easily fool yourself. This is incredibly easy to do if you're single when you start. 'It's just a bit of fun,' you'll think. 'I'll do this for a while and see what happens. If it's hell, I can always stop.'

You see what's happening? You are dipping one toe into the waters of chastity, while keeping the rest of your body on dry land. You're starting the process, but only with a built-in excuse for stopping. The truth is, this isn't just a bit of fun. It's the quickest, easiest way to radically improve your dating life. You're going to have so much more fun being courted properly by adoring men than you've ever had by bonking on the third date with someone you don't completely know and trust.

Don't think of it as 'Something I'll do till something better comes along'. This *is* the better thing that's come along! Celebrate this new chapter in your life. Get behind it, get on top of it – you might as well be getting on top of something. Have some T-shirts printed up with 'No Willy, No Cry' on the front. Tell yourself, 'I'm not going to shag again until I'm 100 per cent secure about where my relationship is going! I'm fabulous and I deserve to be wooed and courted.' Repeat as necessary.

Stage Two: Anger

You know you've hit the Anger stage when you find yourself tutting loudly at couples you see kissing in public. 'Oh yes, it's okay for YOU,' you think, watching her giggle as his hand caresses her bum. 'Yeah, yeah, flaunt your sex life, why don't you. Well, I hope you get herpes, you harlot!'

You might also listen to your friends describe their steamy dates and get unreasonably jealous. It'll suddenly seem like the whole world is off having a marvellous time leaping into bed willy-nilly, while you only get to go home early on Friday nights and feed your hamster.

You might also start to replay old relationships in your head and completely re-write them. The heartbreaking tale of *Ben And How I Discovered He Was Cheating On Me With Emma* will become the Hallmark-channel film *Wonderful Ben, Whose Sexuality Was So Strong, He Needed Two Women To Fulfil Him, And That's Perfectly Understandable And Really Quite Modern.*

All I can say to you is, wait. This stage passes really quickly. It'll help to remind yourself that your past affairs weren't perfect because they all ended. And that your friends' relationships aren't always perfect either. And couples who snog in the street aren't lust-crazed and blissful – they just can't afford a hotel.

Stage Three: Bargaining

'Dear God, if I can just have one night of passion with my last-but-one ex Jason, I promise I'll spend the rest of my life actually reading your book and trying not to covet stuff.'

Slap yourself.

Stage Four: Depression

During this stage, you might start to feel like giving up on men and love forever. Be careful – while these thoughts are normal, they might easily spiral downwards. 'Oh what's the point of boyfriends?' could turn into 'Oh, what's the point of leg-shaving?' and end up in, 'Oh, what's the point of showers?'

You'll find yourself slumping around in old tracksuits, not meeting anyone's eye and exhibiting a general air of someone who, a month later, is found eaten to death by their cat.

Is this bad? Hell, no! Who's going to bonk you when you look like this? This actually makes celibacy a walk in the park. A walk where everyone takes care to avoid you and doesn't want to get down-wind.

The important thing to remember is, it's not a lack of sex that's making you feel down, it's just the big change you've taken on. The honest truth is, for most women, great sex is NOT a guarantee of happiness. It can feel like it, but if the rest of the relationship is wonky, sex is not enough to keep you on top of the world. In fact, if you ever found yourself thinking, 'Well, sex is the only thing I'm getting from this relationship,' you know you ought to stop. All the time you're having sex with someone like this, you're stopping yourself meeting someone better. Not just for those two and a half minutes you're actually doing the dirty deed, but the rest of the time that any of your mental energy is revolving round the wrong man. You won't be looking for anyone else, you won't experience that uplifting, 'I'm single and ANYTHING is possible!' feeling.

To get you through this bit, get regular exercise – of the upright variety – make sure you don't stop answering your phone, and be nice to yourself. Massages help a lot, because they give you the skin-on-skin contact you're missing. And keep your chin up, because tomorrow could bring . . .

Stage Five: Acceptance

You've made it! Acceptance is an unexciting word for a stage which feels so lovely. You'll feel calm, in control, and finally able to give Abstinence a really good go. You'll be looking at your old relationships with 20/20 vision, and feeling really quite good about your future. This stage is wonderful and will last approximately up until the time a sexy new man puts his tongue in your mouth. So enjoy it while you can.

Know What You Want

Another way to boost your resolve is to be really clear on why you are trying out this new way of dating. Obviously you're doing it because you want to be in a really happy, secure relationship that is leading to commitment. But to get that kind of relationship, you have to be able to recognize it when you see it.

This would be the perfect time to write your personal Man-Mission Statements to yourself. In a notebook, write five things you are not willing to compromise on in your next relationship. Things like, 'I will not tolerate infidelity, flakiness, unreliable men, stinginess and crappy Valentine's Days.' Then write down what you DO want. 'I want an adorable man who makes me laugh, rings me every day and doesn't buy my birthday present at any shop that also sells milk,' for example. Be specific, because until you know what you want, you'll never find it.

You could also try some Feng Shui cures for your love life. Even if, like a certain sceptic I know, you think Feng Shui should be renamed F'ing Shite, it can still be a way to improve your love life for the simple reason that it makes you *focus* on it. So many of us approach our love lives with the attitude, 'If it happens, it happens.' We never do that when it comes to our career, our money, or getting dressed in the morning, so why do we leave one of the most important parts of our life to chance?

So, stand in your bedroom with your back to the door. See the far right-hand corner? That's your Relationship corner. Bad things to find here would be the bin, a dirty linen-basket and/or your ex boyfriend. Clear any of those out, give the space a good clean, and add a pair of red or pink candles, a photograph of a happy couple, and a mirror.

You can also write a Cosmic Shopping List of things you'd like the Universe to bring you. My best friend did this before she met her husband, and he was exactly what she asked for, right down to his black hair, blue eyes, and sense of humour. Sadly, her list was short and didn't include 'Earns a fortune, loves exotic holidays, hates football'. So write a *detailed* description of your ideal man, hide it somewhere in that far-right corner of your bedroom and trust that the perfect man will find you.

Use the Buddy System

It'll be a big help if you can enlist a friend in your new no-nookie dating regime. For one thing, you can boost each other's resolve at tricky moments of weakness. And for another, you can always console yourself with the fact that she isn't getting any either.

Having a partner-in-virtue will also help prevent your other friends from accidentally weakening your resolve. Despite the fact that every woman instinctively knows casual sex is *not* the yellow-brick road to happiness, we give each other hopeless relationship advice like, 'Oh go on, I would,' 'I shagged David on the first date and we turned out okay – well, till the divorce,' and 'But you might be run over by a bus tomorrow. Why not just have a bit of fun?'

The motive behind these statements is sweet – every woman wants to see her friends happy. It's also a lot more fun to give out light-hearted, 'Do it! Do him!' advice than to stand there like Grandma, insisting you sleep with your hands on top of the duvet.

Find a friend who wants the same things from life that you do, and promise to back each other up. Vow to each other that you'll always be on the end of the phone to talk the other one down from any erect willy, any time.

How Not to Have Sex – When You're Dating

Oh, it's a breeze to be chaste when you're single, and the only action you're getting is the occasional mammogram. But what do you do when you meet a new man? Worse than that, a good-looking new man? Worse than THAT, a good-looking, sexy man who kisses like a dream, makes you laugh, and seems to find you trouser-tentingly arousing in return? It's easier than you think. Here's what to do, and what not to do.

First Date

Depending on your past, and how much trouble you've been getting yourself into before, this date may or may not be a testing time. I think for most of us it won't be, because we all know that we shouldn't sleep with men on the first date. After that, of course, all bets (and pants) are off.

However, now you've taken your vow of chastity, you'll probably feel differently about this date. You'll either feel self-conscious and nervous – so focussed on not shagging him that you'll scream like Rain Man if he puts his hand on your arm – or you'll feel the need to go confessional, and tell him over the starters that he's not going to be getting lucky any time soon.

Relax. No man expects to get lucky on the first date. In fact, contrary to what they'd have us believe, no man EXPECTS to get lucky on ANY date unless money has changed hands. Men know that the woman is in the driving-seat when it comes to sex.

Feel better? Okay, good.

No Setting the Date

The next thing to remember on the early dates, is that you *don't* have to tell him you're not going to shag him for a while. You don't have to go into the reasons why, and you don't have to give him an estimated time-line of when he might get some lovin'. No spreadsheets, no whore-oscopes – 'If we see each other three times a week, with sexual action increasing in intensity at the rate of five per cent each time; barring any setbacks over Valentine's Day, I'd expect us to be getting dirty around 29 October. That all right with you?'

Yes, you might feel guilty when he's sitting there being all amusing over dinner and you're looking at him, thinking, 'You *so* wouldn't be laughing if you knew how long it's going to be before you get any.' But you have no reason to feel guilty. In fact, you should feel like you're doing him a favour. Men prefer to chase. They prefer the anticipation of sex, to feel like they're earning something that doesn't get handed out to every man who buys you a drink.

Instead of telling him your secret plan not to bonk him, you can show him through your actions that it's not on the cards. You can kiss him goodnight at the front door, and not invite him in for coffee. You can keep kissing as just kissing, and not let his hands wander over you like he's blind.

You can also respond in the right way to any sexual innuendoes. Men make off-colour comments on the first few dates as a way to (if you'll excuse the expression) 'feel you out' about sex. You'll notice this if you look for it. Within the first couple of dates, a man (especially if he's inexperienced) will bring up the subject of sex and watch to see how you react. The right response is not to laugh along in a matey, boys-together way. It's to change the subject.

If he makes a rude joke that's hilarious, and you can't help but laugh as your sense of humour is rather locker-room too, that's okay, but don't try to out-do him with some filthy jokes of your own. And don't talk about your sex life before him. Not now, and not later.

The Conversation

Of course, you will eventually have to tell him that you're not the type to leap into bed with him quickly. When's the right time to bring it up? When he does. Every man has a personal Shag Calendar and it's different with each bloke, depending on his past experiences, his self-confidence, the types of girls he usually dates, etc. And so you don't want to steam in there on Date Three, saying all dramatically, 'I want you to know that I'm not Speedy Gonzales when it comes to full penetration, so if all you're looking for is sex, you'd better leave now!' when, actually, he wasn't expecting to get lucky for at least another year.

If you leave it till he mentions it, it's like you weren't even thinking about tactically avoiding having sex with him. Then you can react in a better way. 'Oh. Wow. Um, you know, I haven't really thought about why we haven't shagged yet. Hmm.' Throw in a few puzzled-looking forehead creases and he'll back-pedal wildly, thinking he's put his foot in it.

If he sits silently, obviously expecting a full breakdown on the Sex Situation, you can say something like, 'I'm not really into having casual sex. I prefer to wait until I know where things are going.' Keep it light, don't metaphorically roll your sleeves up to settle in for a good long *discussion* about it. Men love discussions with us because they're hoping to change our minds. This is something you're doing because it feels right. It's not something he can logically debate you out of until you announce, 'You have changed my mind! Please unhook my bra and let the mating commence!'

Instead, if you say, 'I prefer to wait until I know where things are going,' you are cleverly telling him that a: you are looking for a serious relationship (this will not scare him off, it will make him think you are the type of girl men have serious relationships with, even if, in fact, pints of milk last longer than your average affair); b: he will have to continue to impress you if he wants to ever get lucky; and c: this is something you have done before. That is important. If you show weakness, he will go in for the kill and use all his moves to manoeuvre you into a new position, preferably horizontal.

His reactions to this statement are telling, too. If he likes you, he'll smile (even if it kills him) and say something supportive. But if he's a player, he'll try to undermine you. Or worse, he'll ask you if you've had some kind of 'bad experience' in your past. Please. Like you must have been molested by your nursery teacher not to want to *leap* into bed with this jackass?

If he says that, reply, 'No – but you're about to have one if you're not careful' and change the subject.

The most important thing to get right is your attitude. If you appear confident and secure with your no-nookie decision, he'll accept it. If you seem apologetic or open to persuasion, he'll keep bringing it up, again and again. Which will be about as sexy as being trapped in a lift with a traffic warden with halitosis.

Forget the Third Date Rule

Sex this early in a relationship – and the third date IS early, you could rack-up three dates in a weekend – is not as expected as you'd think. Sex within three dates is always just a bonus in the male mind. And not even a bonus that they value, because it came so easily that they don't feel they really earned it.

Think of Prince Charming in Cinderella. Did he get to ream her pumpkin after taking her out three times? Nooo. He had to search the kingdom, getting every woman to try on the glass slipper. That took commitment. I bet when he found Cinders at the end, he really felt like he'd won something. Now compare that to a man who has called you a couple of times and sprung for three evenings out, and gets rewarded with a shag. Do you feel he has the same sense of air-punching achievement? That feeling he's conquered Everest? Do you think that he even knows you yet? You'd freak if a man told you he loved you after three dates. You'd think it was pretty shallow, and probably lust, and you'd be right. But lust goes away as soon as it's satisfied. When it's *not* satisfied, it can grow into something deeper.

So – keep just kissing him goodnight at the front door, and shoo him away if he makes noises about coming in. You can do it. Don't worry that he won't think you like him. If you're friendly on the dates, compliment him on what a lovely time you've had, and seem to like kissing him (*note: you don't have to grind into his pelvis to show you like kissing him. The simple fact that you're not wiping your mouth on your sleeve and dry-heaving shows you like it*), he'll know enough.

It's Only Different Because You Like Him

When you meet someone you really like, it's easy to see him as different. You're scared of losing him, so you use everything you can to keep him, including sex. You think you'll hook him in with amazing nookie and then he'll be yours forever.

I wish this worked – think of the fun we'd have! – but it doesn't. Really, what you have between your legs is the same as every other woman has, and even if yours blows bubbles and picks up satellite TV, it's still not the reason a man will stay with you. But a man can get hooked on you if you *don't* sleep with him, because then you become a challenge and a mystery; a puzzle he wants to solve.

Dinner at His Place

After four or five sex-free dates, he'll bring out the big guns. Instead of drinks or a movie, you'll be invited to … Dinner at His Place. Is he trying to wow you with his Smeg and his ability to put some meat in the oven? Well, yes, in a manner of speaking. Basically, men ask you over for dinner because their kitchen is a lot closer to their bedroom than any restaurant. They imagine the whole scenario – Barry White on the stereo, Jamie Oliver on the plates, you on the waterbed.

I strongly advise you to sweetly decline this offer. When you like a man, it's hard enough to refuse his advances without putting yourself seconds from his bedroom when you've had a few glasses of wine. Say something vague like, 'Oh, that sounds fab, but not this time'. You don't have to give your reasons – he knows what you mean.

Dinner at Your Place

You might not be Waiting Until Marriage To Have Sex, but I think you should be Waiting Until Marriage To Start Cooking. Make a mental vow: if he doesn't put a ring on your hand, you're not going to put an oven-glove on it. Dating is not a time to showcase your domestic goddess skills and beat him into submission with an egg whisk. Cooking is way too nurturing and caring, and before you know it you're cutting up his steak and burping him.

In fact, ideally you should avoid having him spend too much time at your place for any reason, at least for the first month. This is easy if you live with your parents and your Dad has put a snooker-style 'one foot must be on the floor at all times' rule on your bedroom, but much harder if you live with flatmates or alone. Worth it, though.

Why?

Hanging around your place on dates means he's not taking you out and showing you off, which is the least you deserve when you're dating. Trust me, when you get married you'll spend more time at home than a pot plant, so get out while you still can.

Long slow kisses lead to him slipping a hand under your shirt, which leads to you straddling him seductively, which leads to him popping your jeans button, which leads to you sexily taking off your bra, which leads to him snogging your boobs, which leads to you both being chucked out of the restaurant. But if you're at home, nobody is there to throw buckets of water over the pair of you, so you end up humping like happy hippos. That's all fine when you're in a long-term relationship, but NOT in the first month of dating. So no hang-out, DVD dates for you yet, missy.

Things get emotionally heavier on at-home dates too. You wear comfier clothes, drink more, and generally spill your guts much more easily than you would if you had other people sitting three feet from you on both sides. One minute you're reading him passages from your favourite books, the next you're opening up to him about how you've had therapy for five years. It's all too much. Stay outside, where he'll be trying to keep your attention, not looking at you and thinking, 'Man, this girl can talk.' If you have too many at-home dates, it's only a matter of time before he sees that fat photo of you in a bikini on the fridge with the urgent caption, 'THIS IS WHAT CHOCOLATE DOES', or glances at your bookcase bulging with titles like *Extreme Cellulite – How To Hide It* and *Get Any Man To Propose Within The Hour*.

Men tend to want what they can't have. And if you're

spending all your time together, cosied up on the sofa, wrestling over the remote control, he won't feel the urgent need to see you all the time, live with you or marry you. Because, oh look – there you are! And at-home dates are often interrupted by your phone, or your washing-machine – your life doesn't stop just because he's there – so before you know it you're scrubbing the bath in front of him, and discussing the best way to get fake-tan stains out of your underwear. It's hardly *Casablanca*. If you're a real home-body, just bear in mind that this is only for the first few weeks. And anyway, why are you so keen to show off your house? Do you really think any man fell in love with a woman for her home-made curtains and witty furniture arrangements? Do you think blokes fantasize about interior designers? This is you wanting to open up too much. Remember, you should be practising the art of Being Mysterious. He should be *dying* to see where you live. And the longer it takes him to get access to your place, the more he'll appreciate it.

Listen, if the urge gets almost uncontrollable, just don't clean your house before he picks you up. It's the residential version of wearing Period Knickers.

Don't Tease

One of my friends, Julia, was on her fourth date with her now-husband Chris, and they were snogging behind a pub. (Classy.) He was kissing her neck and she moaned in ecstasy.

He stopped, lifted his head and said, 'I'm getting really mixed messages here.'

Eh? Mixed messages? They were BEHIND A PUB. Any minute a barman was going to come round the corner with a crate of empties – what did Chris think, that Julia was going to fall to the floor and ravish him to the sound of Pale Ales crashing into the recycler?

This is an example of how men will desperately look for the go-ahead at any time. You say, 'Do you fancy a coffee?' He hears, 'Come in and I'll ask my flatmate to join us.' You say, 'You're a really sexy kisser', he hears 'Do me till I bleed!'

So, for the first month at least, don't let your snogging sessions get out of hand. Kissing outside is *usually* safe, so enjoy your goodnight kisses to the full. But don't start grinding against him, grabbing anything, or trying to work out how big he is with your hand (too professional). All this behaviour is telling a man that you're up for it, now. And men listen to actions, so your no-sex speech will count for nothing if you start squirming against him like a pole-dancer.

If you let him come into your home, straddle him passionately, and don't stop his hands when they go under your waistband, he will get annoyed when you later try to end the session without sex. And you know what? He'll have a right to feel like that. You can't get him all worked up and then expect him to jump off you happily with a smile when you figure things have gone far enough.

So, for the first month, only goodnight kisses. (Don't whine

– remember how sexy these were when you were fifteen? They're just as sexy now.)

Second month – above the clothes. Third month – above the clothes. Fourth month – above the clothes.

Only at the time he's said 'I love you' and *proved* it with his actions, should you start having Oral Pleasure. Yes, I know this is horrific but you have to trust me that he'll say 'I love you' a lot sooner when you date my way. When you're sleeping with men, dating loses its intrigue and things can stretch out to years. My way, they happen quickly. (See the Success Stories chapter for proof.)

Another reason why I don't want you giving or receiving oral sex without some declaration of his feelings *first* is that once you hit Third Base, a Home Run is pretty much around the corner. You might be the type of girl who can enjoy oral sex without desperately wanting a good banging afterwards but I never was, and I know that as soon as you're both naked and his mouth is all over your nethers, your resolve will snap and – oops!

Full sex should only happen when you've got what you want: commitment, engagement or marriage.

The good thing about this way of dating is that you'll really *know*. It's not like the 'I really hope this is going somewhere' kind of relationships you have when you leap into bed quickly. No more of those agonizing, two-year affairs where you're scared to mention The Future, or you secretly check his internet Favourites to see if he's still on Match.com. In the old-fashioned way of dating, men open up sooner and give you that blissful feeling of being cherished, secure and safe. And *then* you can shag his head off. And – you know what? – he'll probably send you flowers afterwards.

Question Time!

I can't do without my vibrators – are you insane? What will I do without some form of release? How can pleasuring myself be wrong?

I know this sounds unbearable, and you're terrified you'll roam round Waitrose eyeing up the marrows, but just try it for a month. If you don't find that your sex-drive has calmed down by then, you have my permission to crack open your bedside drawer and use up ten AA batteries in one night. All I'm saying is that, without regular stimulation, your libido will settle down into a gentler phase. Men are different – they get hornier the longer it's been, but we tend to go the other way. At the moment you feel like you'll never make it through a week without getting a Buzz, but when was the last time you tried?

It's obviously better to masturbate than it is to pick some random man to shag, so if you find it unbearable, go for it. But try a tingle-free month. Please? For me? It's one of the best ways to boost your creative energy and regain some mental space from thoughts about sex. It's also good to wean yourself off a toy (they can be addictive, and de-sensitize you), and ensures that, when you are in a sexual relationship again, you'll really enjoy yourself.

My friends think I'm crazy. They all sleep with their boyfriends and they're in great relationships.

I'm not dooming you to a lifestyle straight out of *The Sound of Music*. I just want you to see that until there is definite commitment, and the man is in love with you, you will have a better time if you don't jump into bed. You can't use your friends' relationships as a barometer for yours. Maybe they want different things than you do – this book is specifically for women who are searching for commitment and courtship. Besides, there's a reason you've read this far. Deep-down, do you think casual sex has worked out for you? If you're trying to hold off now, do you feel different in yourself – happier, less tense, more confident? Having sex will not make a man fall in love with you, or guarantee you a wonderful relationship. But not having sex too soon will weed out the lazy, not-bothered men quicker than gunning them down with an AK-47. When you do find your perfect match and bonk him, you'll find that your relationship stays romantic and passionate for a long time. Then your friends might start envying you.

This was all fine till I bumped into my ex and had sex with him. He now wants us to be 'Friends With Benefits'. Is this bad?

It doesn't take women very long to see the loophole in this plan – that men you've already slept with seemingly 'don't count', and appear to be the perfect solution, as No-Strings Lovers. A good idea? Well, let's see. Having passionate nookie with a man who doesn't want to be in a relationship with you anymore – does this sound confidence-boosting? Ah, but you don't want to be in a relationship with him either. Er, so why are you boffing him? That evening you spend getting dressed up, cleaning your flat and jumping all over your ex could be spent out on the town, meeting new men. It doesn't seem like a waste of much time – after all, it's only one night a week, or after a night out – but it's stopping you focussing on your goal, which should be *meeting someone better*. Sometimes you need to feel lonely to actually be motivated to make changes in your life. Cosy evenings in with your ex, or another casual partner, will be evenings you don't spend writing an online-dating advert or signing up for speed dating, or writing a novel, or revamping your wardrobe. ... But take the sex temporarily out of your life and you will have whole evenings to fill. As a friend of mine once said, 'No-strings lovers are the marijuana of relationships – they sap you of your ambition.'

♥

Should I mention my views on sex in my online-dating advert?

God no! Don't mention anything about sex online, ever, unless you want to be besieged with photos of men's erections. Some sites have a section where you can reveal how sexually adventurous you are – don't answer.

♥

My friend, who has been my 'buddy', has fallen off the wagon and bonked her new man. She seems happy – it's weakening my determination.

Of course she's happy! She's like a dieter who has run laughing and screaming into a Häagen Dazs factory. But she's not really giving this a chance to work, she's just falling back into her old habits. Think of this as an experiment you're doing – you're going to see if you enjoy life better without casual sex. Have some self-discipline, woman.

I'm normally good at holding off but with my new boyfriend, I'm really tempted. I don't think I can wait much longer, but he hasn't said he loves me or mentioned our future. Help!

The reason you want to boff him is probably *because* he hasn't said he loves you or mentioned your future. You feel a bit unsure, so you're looking for a way to bring you both closer together. Sex feels like the perfect solution. But keep your knickers on – if you sleep with him, do you think you'll feel any calmer than you do now? Or do you think you'll be wondering even more fervently how much he likes you, if he loves you, where he sees things going? In the false intimacy after sex, you might even find yourself asking him out loud. Don't do it. Hang in there and watch his actions. If he genuinely cares, he'll confess it soon enough. And if he doesn't, you'll find it much easier to get over the ending of the relationship if you remain resolutely un-rogered.

When I told a bloke that I was holding off on sex, he looked at me oddly and hasn't rung since. Will this happen with everyone?

Only the men who aren't that keen on you. This is a *good* thing that's happened – you wasted, what, a month on this man? If you'd started giving him sex, he'd have stuck around for so much longer. Why isn't that a good thing? Because he *still* wouldn't have cared that much, and you'd have been far more invested in him and the relationship when it eventually finished. Any man who ditches you for not putting out isn't interested in *you*, he's interested in sex. That's why he leaves, to pursue his goal of sex with somebody else. Any man who is interested in you will stick around, to see more of you. If the more of you that he sees happens to be naked and covered in whipped cream, that's only a bonus, and one for which he'll be happy to wait.

♥

Couldn't a bloke lie about loving me, just to get me into bed?

I don't subscribe to the notion that men are liars and cheats. In my experience, men are usually incredibly honest about things, only women choose not to hear them. It is very rare that a man would go through an elaborate charade of dating you for months only to get in your pants. If he is really only after sex, he will quickly end a nookie-free relationship in favour of an easier lay. But if he's undecided, he might stick around a bit longer to see what happens. He will be more intrigued by you than by other girls.

♥

Surely my BF will think I'm inexperienced if I say I usually prefer to wait. I'm in fact very experienced and pride myself on being great in bed. I want him to know how good I am!

Why? Love is not retail. You are not trying to out-sell yourself against every other woman in the world. This kind of attitude is desperate. Your thinking is all, 'Look at me! See how hot I am! I can do back-flips on to the mattress! I could suck a watermelon through a straw! Aren't I better than those other girls?'

Sexual compatibility is important to men, but if he likes you, he'll like you doing stuff to him. He'll get aroused because it's *you* fumbling under his belt buckle, not because you've dislocated your thumb and put apricot jam on your fingers.

He'll realize you're good in bed by how well you kiss him, how your hands move over his back, how skilfully you (eventually) stroke his bits and pieces. And of course, when you finally shag him. Before you're in a secure relationship with him, why should you even be worried? *You* know you're good in bed. He can get to find out, when he's earned the right.

3

Your Extreme Dating Makeover

Everyone probably thinks that I'm a raving nymphomaniac, that I have an insatiable sexual appetite, when the truth is I'd rather read a book.

Madonna

Few women are born slutty; most of us have sluttishness thrust upon us. How? Well, in extreme cases, bad early experiences will lower a girl's self-esteem so drastically that she ends up feeling that her sexuality is all she has to offer men. If you feel this is you (and you'll know if it is), then this book will offer you some support, but not as much as you need. I'm hopeless in a crisis, really, so I would urge you to seek counselling.

The rest of us fall into two camps: we're either Worryingly Spineless or we are naively willing to believe Bad Dating Advice. In this chapter I will rebuild you.

Brittle Backbone Disease

The most common reason for having too-soon sex is out of the fear that, if you don't, your boyfriend will get bored and find someone else. (Actually, no. That's the most *usual* reason. The most *common* reason for having too-soon sex is to get pregnant and therefore bumped up the council-house queue.)

That fear comes from Brittle Backbone Disease. This is an epidemic that is sweeping the country among single twenty- and thirty-something females, and can tragically go undetected for years. But you can do a simple at-home test to see if you're at risk.

Brittle Backbone Disease Diagnostic Screening

Tick any statement that applies to you.

1. You have sent flowers to a man who wasn't in a coffin about to be buried.
2. You often feel a slight sense of resentment that men never do as many thoughtful and/or romantic things for you as you do for them.
3. When you ask a man, 'Where is this going?', you're not usually talking about the car.
4. You believe in reciprocity, and don't mind going Dutch on dates.

5. You accept Booty Calls.

6. You have done late-night drive-bys past a man's house.

7. You have baked for a male to whom you did not actually give birth. (Earn five bonus points if you iced his name on the top. Earn 150 bonus points if you delivered it to his work.)

8. You have tidied up a man's house – where you do not also reside – without being asked.

9. During that ad hoc cleaning session, you either read his diary, looked through his photograph albums and/or read letters in his private collection that weren't sent from you. Earn 100 bonus points if you later mentioned doing this to him, and got a bit weepy.

10. You have watched a man play sport more than twice. Earn twenty bonus points if it was raining. Earn 500 bonus points if he hadn't actually asked you to come.

Results:

- If you ticked between one and five statements, you have early-stage Brittle Backbone Disease. This is good news, as Brittle Backbone Disease caught this early can often be completely cured.

- Between six and twenty points; you have mild Brittle Backbone Disease. You will need treatment, but the outlook is still good for a full recovery.

- More than twenty-one points and you are suffering from critical Brittle Backbone Disease and it will be having major effects on the health of your relationships. You might also find it hard to stand up for yourself, or just to stand up at all.

Why it's not Nice to be Nice

I know that 'nice' sounds like a lovely thing to be in relationships. It's like, 'Yes, I'm nice. What's the alternative? Chop his nuts off in his sleep?' And you're right that being *sweet* and *charming* and *kind* is lovely in relationships. But often, being 'nice' actually means, 'I'm going to give and give until you realize how much I adore you.' Is this a good dating strategy? Nope. Why not? Because it doesn't work.

When you give a lot, you're sending the message that you don't really feel you're loveable on your own. You, just you – unencumbered with romantic cards, presents, or a Japanese sexual technique involving back-flips – are not worthy of being adored, so you make up for the shortfall by adorning yourself with extra stuff. This is a terrible thing to think, and a terrible thing to allow others to think about you.

Also, it's relatively easy to get into the habit of 'giving to receive'. This is when you send someone a present because you would actually like to receive a present from them. You think, 'Well, I'll go first – I'll send him a sweet card and then he'll realize I'm a sweet-card kind of girl, and then *he'll* send *me* sweet cards.' Do you see what I mean? In order to kick-start the romantic presents, you make the first move.

But this doesn't work either. In the end, all that happens is that you feel resentful, lonely, and you run out of stamps.

This resentment will build until you either end the relationship or ditch the too-niceties and get into the habit of only giving *back*. This sends a much better message. It says, 'I'm nice to you when you're nice to me.' Which is a good way of ensuring a man keeps treating you well.

Of course you can give in relationships, but I don't recommend it in the beginning. You don't need to in the beginning, it's a waste of your time. At the start of relationships, a man is all geared up to try to impress you. When you jump in there and start trying to impress him instead, he stops his pursuit. We'll cover more on this later.

Nice Girls Don't, but Too-Nice Girls *Do*

As well as giving too much in relationships in the form of time, attention and presents, women suffering from Brittle Backbone Disease also give too much, too soon in bed. It's for the same reason – if you don't think that you are enough by yourself to guarantee a man comes back for another date, it's tempting to chuck in a quick blowjob to seal the deal.

Does this work? Well, yes – if you want a man to keep coming back for just your blowjobs. Do you?

You don't need to 'give' to a man sexually to ensure he comes back for more. In fact, it's much, much better if you don't. We've already seen how delayed rewards boost dopamine stores in the brain, so a man will feel the sex is better the longer he's had to wait for it. If you start popping your jawbone on the first date, he'll like it at first but quickly start to become complacent and picky. Soon his delighted squeals of 'My God, you have no gag reflex – you're a medical marvel!' will change to criticisms like, 'Can't you gargle the *Football Focus* theme tune before you swallow?'

You'll soon feel you have to work even harder to impress him. Before you know it, you'll be buying sex manuals by the caseload just to find something you can give him that no other woman has. That's good news for people like me who write sex manuals, but bad news for people like you who have to shell out money just to ensure Mr Cocky keeps coming back for something complicated and dangerous.

If you want to give him something he's never had before, give him the thrill that comes from making him wait to have sex with you.

Feel the Fear and Don't do it Anyway

If you're suffering from Brittle Backbone Disease, holding back on humping will really boost your confidence. It's hard to doubt a man's interest in you when he keeps on seeing you despite the fact that he's getting as much action as the Pope. That raises your self-esteem. You are probably used to giving to men to keep them around. So when you don't give them anything, their continued attraction is like having a billboard erected inside your house that says, 'You're Fabulous!'

Also, men treat women differently before they've had sex with them. They're more attentive, sweeter, and more on-edge. They haven't relaxed yet. It's wonderful to be on the receiving end of that kind of attention. You might think you prefer a racier, more confident man who keeps you guessing but, again, that could simply be a symptom of Brittle Backbone Disease. Instead of welcoming devoted men, you feel put off by them. They seem like over-eager puppies and after a while you have a terrible urge to leave them by a motorway. You'll know this is you if you always find keen men unattractive. I'm not talking about seriously over-affectionate men who profess love on the first date, ring you twenty-five times a day and propose when you're trying to dump them – they'd put *anyone* off. But just run-of-the-mill, reliable and dependable men. If they put you into a coma, you might have self-esteem issues. You can't love anyone who loves you, because deep down you feel unworthy of it. It causes Impostor Syndrome, that one day your man will find out how horrible you *really* are and immediately chuck you. Because of this, you might find yourself deliberately sabotaging relationships so you can hurry up and get to the dumping stage before you're committed.

This can end up being your pattern. But if you break that pattern by withholding sex in your next relationship, you'll keep a clearer head.

Bad Dating Advice

In a perfect world, none of us would need to read a book like this to discover that shagging a man in the taxi back from a first date probably isn't the *best* idea. In a perfect world, we'd all be lofty love goddesses who strut the streets like supermodels, and turn down dates from anyone who doesn't already adore us.

However, life isn't perfect and we do need books to give us a nudge occasionally. And do you know why? Because the advice given in most young girls' magazines is hopeless. If I hadn't actually worked in women's magazines, I'd be convinced their offices were actually just stuffed with men, all plotting together to further favoured male causes like *Let's All Go Dutch on Dates!* and *Nothing Says 'I Love You' Like a Threesome.*

What else could be the reason behind the terrible advice that is doled out to us from the time we are old enough to buy our first copy? If you think I'm being harsh, let's take a quick look at the advice being dished out to teenagers:

Dear Girl's Mag,

I'm sixteen and have been going out with my boyfriend for two months. He's keen to, as he says, 'move our relationship to the next level'. I'm curious to try sex too, but don't have anyone to talk about it with.

Dear Curious,

Do you have a friendly teacher in your school to talk to? Discussing it with them might be helpful. If you're in a steady relationship, it's natural to be curious about sex. Just be sure that you sort out your contraception first – your doctor should be able to help.

Argh! No mention of the fact that this girl has been seeing her boyfriend for roughly one summer holiday. Just go ahead and make sure you have contraception, because nothing matters as long as you don't get yourself knocked up. Forget the fact that your boyfriend sounds like a smooth-talking manipulator who just wants to brag to his mates that he went all the way with you – chat to someone at school. Yup, that's gonna happen, isn't it. 'Miss, I'm sorry I haven't finished my coursework but I was rogering my boyfriend behind the youth club. Do you think this is okay, by the way? We've been together for two months.' Grrr.

None of us will ever succeed in the dating world with advice like this still hanging around in the back of our minds, like a secretly lesbian flatmate who looks like she means well but who is, in fact, trying to scupper our chances of ever meeting anyone decent.

The reason *behind* this advice is good. The women writing for younger titles are trying to empower girls, and give them the feeling that the world is their oyster. Only, when you chase boys, ask them out and bonk them after two months, you quickly find the world isn't your oyster – it's just a nasty case of crabs. And the worst part is, girls are usually born with a perfectly feisty attitude. Little girls are natural flirts. They bat their eyelashes, wear pretty dresses and run away squealing the minute a boy approaches them. You don't see little girls moodily walking round the playground discussing the benefits of 'equal relationships'. Left untouched, none of us would dream of chasing a boy. We'd either be off in the stables sighing about a pony, or experimenting with new hairstyles, practising seductive glances and waiting to be approached. But instead, we read stuff like the above and start doubting ourselves.

So, in case you still have any scraps of Bad Teen Advice still lingering in your brain, here is your Deprogramming.

Bad Advice Deprogramming

Bad Advice: 'Follow your heart. Look at Romeo and Juliet!'

Deprogramming: This one is easy. Yes, do look at Romeo and Juliet. Take a good long look. In fact, stand right at their graves and really take it all in. Juliet followed her heart and ended up dead, which sounds romantic but is a bit limiting long term. If she'd used a bit of sense, she would have got over Romeo. It might have taken a few weeks of weeping delicately into a lace handkerchief, but soon she would have picked herself up and gone on to be just as miserable over someone new.

I disagree that women in the full grip of passionate love should be advised to follow their hearts. When we follow our hearts it invariably brings on a coronary. Our hearts are too soft when we're keen on someone, they're full of dreams and hopes and Hollywood endings. They lead us into temptation. Instead we should always be told to use our heads. Success in love usually comes from having the ability to keep our feet on the ground, instead of waving them in the air, and you can only do that if you conduct your relationships *rationally*.

Besides, when someone advises you to 'follow your heart', they don't actually mean that. What they mean is, 'We've been talking about this for ages and I'm a bit bored now, so I'm going to say something pseudo-supportive and friendly sounding, but which ultimately chucks the ball firmly back in your court.'

Not having sex helps you to use your head. No, not in that way – I'm not making a joke about blowjobs. I mean, it's easier to be rational before you've bonked your bloke. As soon as you've had sex with a man, you lose your objectivity. When that happens, you end up doing things which you *think* are following your heart, but are actually just following his penis.

Bad Advice: **Men like women who ask them out! They find it flattering! And feisty!**

Deprogramming: And forward! And frightening! Men don't like women who ask them out. They don't. I'm sorry, I know it's sickening, but they don't. Yes, you know lots of women who asked their boyfriends out and they seem quite happy. Just wait a while. Soon, those same women will be moaning to you about how they've been living with their boyfriend for three years now and he is still avoiding the subject of marriage.

My friend Milena is a perfect example. She spotted her partner Jake across a crowded office and knew instantly that he was The One. She managed to casually get to know him over the next few weeks, then sent him a flirty email suggesting they go out for a drink. He replied (a day later), and they started seeing one another. Fast-forward seven years: Milena and Jake are now living together, and every birthday Milena gets all over-excited about the idea that Jake might finally pop the question. Last year he nearly gave her a heart attack by asking if he could take her to the jewellery shop to pick out a little something. Milena couldn't breathe, and was eyeing up the sparkling rings as they walked towards the shop . . . then Jake firmly pulled her round towards the watches.

Why did this happen? Because Jake never got the chance to 'choose' Milena. He never got the opportunity to spot her first, get to like her, and make his mind up about asking her out for a drink. She did it all for him. Now he has all the time in the world to make up his mind about wanting to marry her.

Instead of asking men out, you have to whet their appetite. You have to appeal to them visually, but keep a bit of mystery and not make it too easy, so they can get the opportunity to long for you. They *love* longing for you. They love the part when they don't know how much you like them. When you ask them out, they never get that chance. All you can do then is desperately back-pedal, and ditch them from time to time to keep them on their toes. It's exhausting.

So, you should never feel you have to make the first move. You don't. And if a man doesn't ask you out, *there is always a good reason*. He might have crippling debts hanging round his neck, he might have a crippled mother hanging round his flat, or he might just not like you that much.

Sorry.

Bad Advice: If you're meant to be together, you'll be together! Love will find a way!

Deprogramming: Actually, this one is kind of okay if it encourages you to take a passive role. Because often things *do* work out when you trust in the Universe and sit back and watch things unfold. This is bad, however, when it encourages you to do daft things with the attitude of, 'Fate will side-step any mistakes I make if my destiny is to end up with this person.' Like your Divine Plan will erase your mistakes with godly Tippex.

Love *will* find a way, but if you start looking for examples you'll see that the Way is usually the same. Man meets Woman. Man likes Woman. Woman, for some reason – either she is a natural lofty love goddess, or (more often) is currently hung up on, or getting over, someone else – isn't quite so into Man, so he has to chase her for a bit before he gets anywhere. Then they get together and Woman is happy to settle down with Man, because he treats her really nicely.

That is usually the Way. If you're finding that your relationships usually go another Way, it's time to review your map.

Bad Advice Reprogramming

Stand by your man, but don't lie down

Like I might have mentioned, not having sex is the best way to catch and keep the man you're interested in. But that doesn't mean you have to be *mean* to him. In fact, you can be sweeter to your man than you probably ever thought possible and not put him off. You just have to be the right kind of sweet.

John T Molloy, author of *Why Men Marry Some Women and Not Others*, interviewed over 2,000 engaged couples coming out of marriage licence bureaux to find out the secrets of their success. And one of the main factors that attracted the men was that the women showed genuine interest in the man's health and happiness. For example, one woman cancelled a date when her then-boyfriend was coming down with a cold. Another encouraged her boyfriend to go back to college. Another didn't mind when her doctor boyfriend didn't have time to see her for a few weeks, instead of sobbing, 'Sod the bypass – my heart is breaking too!' In fact all the women who went on to marry their partners showed a genuine concern for their man's well-being from the start.

But they didn't turn into doormats. *None* of the women ever cooked fancy meals or cleaned their man's home, allowed him to treat them lazily, or put their bloke's hobbies and interests before their own. And when it came to giving, the women usually gave just a little bit *less* than their man.

When in doubt, don't do anything that inconveniences you. And when you look at the examples given above, you can see that while the women's actions were sweet to their partners, they were also self-serving. Cancelling a date with a man who has a cold so he can go home and rest sounds sacrificial, but in reality the woman was probably just ducking a billion germs. Ditto the woman who ended up being a doctor's wife – by telling him to call her when he was free, she was saving herself from dates where he had to rush off, leaving her alone in a restaurant full of people wondering what she'd said. You see? Never let yourself feel that if you don't bend over backwards to please a bloke, he'll chuck you. And talking of bending over backwards, the women who got married had 'almost never' had sex on the first date.

Clever Compliments

Men are suckers for flattery, but they prefer to be complimented on what they *do* rather than what they *are*. (We're the opposite, which is why we often get this one wrong.) In a restaurant, a man would prefer you raved on about how delicious the food is, rather than tell him he's so handsome, he should leave his face to medical science. The food compliment rewards what he has done for you – i.e. picked a good restaurant and not put his thumb over the expensive dishes on the menu. The handsome compliment is nice but he won't feel he's *earned* it. Likewise, he'll love compliments on his body if he's worked out for months to get *GQ*-worthy abdominals, but he'll only feel so-so if you tell him his eyes are the colour of bluebells. Concentrate on what he has done for you. Let him know he makes you happy. It'll encourage him to keep doing it.

Don't Be Little Miss Fix-It

Men, by and large, need more space than Captain Kirk. Let him have it. It will please him. It will please him even more if you give him this space when there has been a problem or a disagreement between you. This can be agony, I know, but in the long run a man prefers to know that you trust him to do the right thing. And he won't get that message if you're constantly suggesting solutions to problems between you.

If, for example, a date ends on a bad note, *resist* the temptation to get home and consult your giant stack of relationship books to come up with a twelve-step rescue regime. Don't stew all night until you feel so guilty and insecure you end up ringing him at 3am to apologize. And don't call him the next morning all casual and light-hearted just so you can secretly suss out if he hates you. Do nothing. Doing nothing is 'working on the relationship' – it's showing him that you trust he will be in touch when he's willing to talk.

This is hard for women because we use communication to solve problems. Men don't, by and large. Or at least not initially. They do like to chat stuff through but only after a prolonged period of gentle contemplation and scratching alone at home first.

Be the Strong, Silent Type

Most dating advice says that the secret of successful relationships is communication. No, it's not. The *real* secret is knowing when to shut up. Behind every successful union is a muzzle. In a study about marriage, researchers from Berkeley University of California found that the longer a couple had been married, the less likely they were to talk about contentious issues in their relationship, or react to negative remarks from one another. They didn't believe they had to, like some relationship experts suggest, write 'love notes' to each other listing exactly how their feelings were hurt when their partner insulted them. They just shut up and put up.

Aah, but you're not the type to put up. You're the type that uses communication to express when she is annoyed about something. Well, good luck with that! I'll see you back here when you realize that men really *don't* listen to a word we say. They listen to what we *do*.

If you're annoyed with your partner, don't stand between him and the TV listing the ways in which he's let you down. He won't take in the words – he'll glance up briefly to see if you're holding a suitcase and, if you're not, he'll go back to the screen. Men know that when we berate them with words we are still investing our time in them. Much more effective is to demonstrate any annoyance with your actions, by walking away to spend time with other people who aren't currently irritating the tits off you.

What you *can* communicate are good feelings. Tell your partner how happy you feel with him, and how great you think things are going. He'll love it (unless he is currently trying to dump you, in which case he will feel quite frightened). The John Gottman Institute in California has proven that it takes FIVE positive interactions between a couple to cancel out ONE bad one. Every time you say 'I love you' or 'Thank you' or 'Great idea!', you are storing good interactions in your 'love bank' which will negate any 'You are such a bloody twat's that accidentally slip out later.

Does this sound a bit keen? Well, it is. But you *can* be keen like this when you're not having sex. You're still not doing the ultimate Keen Thing, which is sleeping with him. So it makes dating a much sweeter experience. You can be warm and effusive and complimentary (about things he does for you) and you will still retain mystery because you're not getting naked and jumping up on top of him. He will hear all your compliments and want to believe they're all true, but he'll retain some doubt because you're not humping him. He'll hear, 'I like you, but . . . I'm not sure I like you enough yet to give myself over to you completely.'

It's this combination of hope plus uncertainty which causes 'limerance'. This term, coined by American psychologist Dorothy Tennov in her 1979 book *Love and Limerance – The*

Experience of Being in Love, is the first stage of infatuation, where you can't eat or sleep or think about anything other than your beloved. It doesn't last long, which is good because it's a nightmare, but it will transform into love (if your affections are returned), or disappear (if they're not). Tennov believed the state of limerance can last from eighteen months to three years, but more recent studies say it can last far longer, and that three years is only the *minimum*. However long it lasts, it's one of the most exciting stages in a relationship. It's agonizing, but often ecstatic.

Act Like a Lady and He'll Behave Like a Gentleman

This is the final part of your Extreme Dating Makeover, and it's an important one. By not having sex with men, you are immediately setting yourself apart from other women. Is that a good thing? I would say 'Fucking right!' but as this is about being more lady-like, let me respond with a dainty nod.

It's wonderful to be different to all the other girls. Men don't crave a woman like every other one they've ever known – they want someone *different*. So *be* different. Don't give up the goods on the first few dates, but more than that, don't ever let him think you are anything less than fabulous. Show him by the way you carry yourself at all times. The easiest way to do this is to be more lady-like, less ladette-like.

No, I'm not sentencing you to a lifetime of Earl Grey tea-sipping, or embroidery. You don't have to be able to pick out a Mozart sonnet on a pianoforte and faint every five minutes. But you can adopt some of the traditional lady-like habits of maintaining mystery, using decorum, and being feminine.

The recent Jane Austen revival shows us that women today are craving a Mr Darcy. We want a manly man who chases us with passionate determination. We want to be chosen and pursued. But you're not going to meet your Mr Darcy unless you start acting like his Lizzie Bennett.

Believe That Men Actually Prefer to Act Like Gentlemen

The first, crucial, step is trusting that men would actually prefer to treat you well. I know that's often hard to believe, as we've all had boyfriends who seem to thrive on forgetting our birthday or turning up three years late for dates. But the truth is, men honestly prefer to treat a woman nicely. Often they're just longing to find the girl who is ballsy enough to demand no less than excellent treatment. So, be that girl.

You'll have seen this before, when a previously Jack the Lad male friend suddenly and unexpectedly smartened up his act when he met a girl he really liked. He decided for himself that he had to behave impeccably or this particular girl wouldn't look twice at him.

Make it easy for a man to treat you well. When you discuss

meeting for a date, ask him, 'What time will you be picking me up?' Don't feel embarrassed or stressed by the question, muttering it with your eyes all squinted-up, in the same tone of voice you'd use to ask a *Big Issue* seller for change from your pound. Instead, say it as if men pick you up for dates all the time. (Even if the only men you have banging on your door are minicab drivers and policemen.) In fact, say it now, out loud:

'What time will you be picking me up?' Get that note of happy expectation in your voice.

'What time will you be picking me *up*?' Not too much – don't go all angry and defensive, like he should be returning a tenner he nicked from you. But just right – confident, yet appreciative.

You can practise saying other things in this voice. 'I see *Pop Idol* clashes with *Top Gear* tonight. Which one shall we watch?' 'Gordon Ramsay just opened a restaurant in our town! Did you still want to get a pizza?'

He will like it when you expect him to be nice to you. It tells him a lot about your dating history – that you are an A-list girlfriend, someone that men treat well.

While I'm nagging you I might as well get all the 'Don'ts' out of the way. Don't remind him about anything. Especially something romantic like Valentine's Day, the anniversary of your first kiss, your pet's operation, or anything else non-practical. When you remind your man about something – especially something romantic – you are sending him two messages: first, that remembering things is not his responsibility, it's yours (which dooms you to a future of buying your own Christmas presents); and secondly, that you don't trust him to remember anything sweet. Men hate not to be trusted.

Instead, with your new ladylike attitude, *expect* him to remember your birthday. Don't micromanage him by writing weekly count-downs to it in his diary. Instead, tell him ONCE that it's your birthday next Thursday, then keep your mouth closed and wait to see what he does. If he forgets it, don't make a big fuss. I mean, obviously start making calls to get him killed, but don't actually tell him you're annoyed. Instead, file it away that this is not a romantic man you're dating, and start deciding whether that will make you miserable long term.

Also, put him in the role of the decision-maker. This is the best way to bring out a man's gentlemanly side. When he asks you what you'd like to do on your date, say, 'You're the best at thinking of good things to do – what are your ideas?' This is good for many reasons. It flatters him and makes him feel important (men often fall in love with women who make them feel good about themselves). And also, it forces him to come up with a date-plan, because he'd never have the guts to say, 'Well, I rather thought I'd wander round to yours after work, grab a shower, a meal and a shag, and then get the last train home while you wash my shirt, so . . . see you at seven?'

Your new attitude should give him the chance to be your hero. If your car broke down, would you sit there glaring at your AA membership card, silently fuming? Or would you,

you know, actually just ring them and give them the opportunity to help? That should be the stance you take with men. Never ignore an opportunity to let your man help you. Not with the basic, day-to-day running of your life – that's your responsibility. But with sudden emergencies, huge spiders or jam-jar lids, you should let men rush to your aid, then thank them happily and graciously.

This all comes naturally when you remind yourself that deep down, a man wants to be the Good Guy to the woman he adores. He wants her to boast about him to her friends, and to have the feeling that he is improving her life.

So, if you give a man countless chances to be lovely to you and he fails, what should you do? Throw him back into the sea. Don't second-guess yourself with thoughts like, 'He didn't realize how important Valentine's Day is for girls,' or 'I'll let him make it up to me at Christmas.' That's just a waste of your time, and it'll only get harder to chuck him as you get more involved. At the first sign of laziness or selfishness, or any kind of general vague feeling that he is on the take, stop taking his calls. He'll either realize how important good behaviour is to you and raise his game (trying to win you back with flowers and presents), or you'll both be free to find someone with whom you're more compatible.

Be Light-Hearted

If there's one thing that's going to guarantee you a happy love-life, it's to not take it seriously. Start thinking about men in old-fashioned terms like 'dalliances' or 'flirtations' to get them in perspective. Minimize the amount of emotional space they take up in your brain.

I'm sure this is one reason why we are all so much better at dating when we're young. We have more going on, we are out all the time, seeing friends, being footloose, and men are just one of the many joys in our lives. Fast-forward to your late twenties and thirties, however, and suddenly there are fewer distractions. As your friends marry off, you have longer, freer weekends stretching ahead of you. Suddenly there are fewer weekends in Ibiza and more weekends in Homebase. Living alone, you think of all the friends you've known, but when you dial the telephone, nobody's home . . .

Thankfully it's all going to be fine. You've taken the first crucial step, by stopping the no-strings nookie. And now anything you do to make your life fun, interesting and busy will boost your ability not to get too hung up on, and moody about, men.

Also, don't spend too much time with men who seem to bring out your more introspective side. Go for the ones who make you feel lighter when you're with them. Why? Because these relationships are usually the ones that are best for you, and tend to have the happiest outcomes. I'm not talking about only going with men who make you laugh. I'm saying, only stay with men in whose company you feel happy and breezy. They're the ones who are good for you. Usually we only feel like this in the company of men who are treating us well, because that feeling of security stops us worrying.

Men will want to be with you if you are happy and cheerful. Even the deepest, most bookish types of men will always prefer the company of someone who seems basically optimistic and light-hearted. I'm not saying you should dampen your brain or hide your intelligence, just don't be a downer. Be charming instead, and make people feel happy when they're with you. Be the type who only passes on compliments about others, not insults. With this kind of attitude you'll be sought out by everyone, and there is nothing more likely to kick-start a man's pursuit than knowing that you are besieged by other people, male or female.

Also, don't use your boyfriend as a sounding board for every problem you have. Instead, rely on your girlfriends, friends and family, at least in the first year of dating. Telling your boyfriend everything you're worried about allows you to start letting friendships slide. It also means you're more likely to feel marooned if the relationship finishes. Suddenly you'll be back to moaning to your friends about the work pressure at your new job, and they'll think, 'What job?'

Don't Flaunt Your Faults

These days, it seems we're all told that the right man will love us despite our faults. I say – bugger that. Do you love the man who confesses he has baffled medical science with his foot-sweat? People tend to fall for those they can admire, so don't ever bring attention to things about yourself that you don't like. I've seen friends go to pieces with men they fancy, and end up confessing that they hate their hands, they took the week off work with menstrual cramps, and that they envy their friend Sarah's skinny thighs.

In books, none of this would matter. In books, the bloke would take our confessional heroine by one of her huge, ugly hands, offer her a hot-water bottle for her PMT and say that he thinks Sarah looks like a chicken. But in real life, men tend to believe what you say about yourself. So our hero would be sitting there, casting discreet glances at my friend's hands, thinking uncomfortably about tampons, and wondering where the lithe-limbed Sarah is.

When someone compliments you, don't get embarrassed and start denying it. Just say, 'Thanks, what a kind thing to say,' and look delighted with them.

Now for Some Questions

Okay, I scored o ticks on the Brittle Backbone Disease screening test. So I can shag anyone, right?

Nope. This just means that you are more of a ball-breaker and have more confidence than some other girls. It won't ultimately affect how men react to you after sex because, as we've seen, men are still genetically programmed to jump and dump.

What if a man asks you to do things for him? Is it okay then?

Yes, but always try to make sure that you are giving less than he asks for. Blokes, by and large, end up falling for women who do less in a relationship because it puts them back into the role of the pursuer. That's where men feel most comfortable. Think about fertility – flowers don't chase bees.

I bought my ex-boyfriend loads of presents and he didn't think it was too nice, he thought it was sweet.

You said 'ex-boyfriend'. QED. Listen up, men won't ever tell you that you're putting them off. Men don't want to hurt your feelings, they just instinctively prefer women who fall into a more feminine role in dating.

I fail to see how a few 'Ooh, you're so strong's will keep a man around who's not getting sex.

It won't keep a man hanging around if he is in short-term mating mode. Researchers at Berkeley discovered that men have two 'pre-sets' for dating – short-term and long-term. When a man is in short-term dating mode, which he typically is when he's a student or just out of a relationship, his objective isn't to meet a wife, it's to sow more oats than a porridge factory. When he's in this mode, you can't get him to commit by complimenting him, shagging him, or doing *anything* to him, so you're right. He will leave you when it becomes clear that your underwear is practically super-glued on. But, when a man is in long-term mode, he will be sufficiently encouraged by your flattering attention to date you *despite* there being no nookie. In fact, long-term men are actually encouraged by chastity, because it shows that you have standards. And because, like we've seen, they believe your actions, the best way to prove to a man that you're not a slut is not to act like a slut. It's not enough to say, 'I don't usually do this.'

♥

Are you sure I can't bake for my boyfriend?

Positive. Just content yourself with the fact that you can make the wedding cake.

♥

You're trying to turn me into an air-head.

No. I just don't want you to appeal too much to his more logical side. If he's a typical man, he'll prefer women who appeal to his right-brain, the side associated with creativity, passion and feelings. Start getting into lengthy political debates on the first few dates and he'll begin to see you as 'buddy' rather than a babe.

It's not a big pain to make my own way to dates. Is letting him pick me up that important?

Yes. If you want a man who cherishes you, you have to leave room for him to cherish you. If you start making fifty per cent of the effort, you'll end up in a fifty/fifty relationship where your man doesn't see you as anything special or out of the ordinary. You'll be more like flatmates. That's not love, it's friendship.

4

Safety in Numbers

Don't put all your eggs in one bastard.

Dorothy Parker

What's the difference between 'dating' and 'being in a relationship'? Sex. Until you've slept with a man, he's not your boyfriend, he's just applying for the position. This brings us to one of the unexpected benefits of sex-free relationships – you can date more than one man at a time.

Nowadays, most of us date nobody for months, then meet some likely-looking dude at a party and fall into being an Insta-Couple. There is a slight grey-area fortnight where neither party knows 100 per cent if they're allowed to accept phone numbers from anyone else, or brush up against people on the bus, but that quickly passes and then the couple carries on dating until they either shack up or split up. But it didn't used to be like this. As early as the 1950s, multiple-dating was the norm in the UK.

When my Mum used to reminisce about her days in the Swinging Sixties when she saw five different men every week, I used to assume she was just – how can I put this nicely? – a slut. But then I asked around with other oldies and they all agreed that dating used to be a much more free and easy activity than it is today.

Except it was far more free than easy – none of these dates included clothing-removal. But when the Pill was launched in the early sixties it was quickly followed by the Sexual Revolution, and multiple-dating was ditched. Dating was replaced with *mating*, and we all ended up as one-man women, which is where we are today.

This isn't the best we can do. Dating one person at once for a long time wastes *years* of your life and your fertility. Plus, we enter into exclusive agreements with men early on, forgoing our chance to compare them with anyone else. And because we're having sex with them – and therefore becoming emotionally involved – we are much more likely to turn a blind eye to any annoying habits that appear later on, because we've already decided to 'make a go of it'.

Don't Rely on Men to Look out for Your Best Interests

Men know that women hold the cards when it comes to sex. They know that it is your choice when sex happens in a relationship. They also know that you'd probably prefer commitment and marriage to a no-strings sexual relationship. They *know* this, so every time you sleep with one, or get into an exclusive relationship without negotiating for a commitment first, *they* realize you're selling yourself a bit short, even if you don't. They feel guilty about it, but figure that it's up to you to look out for your best interests. Just as men are brilliant at looking out for *their* best interests – which are to sleep with as many women as they can before they get saddled with the responsibility of a wife and children.

According to modern dating advice, commitment is something that 'sneaks up' on men. You can't frighten them into it, you have to stealthily stalk them like wildebeest, tiring them out until you can strike when they're at their weakest. I say, nah. Men know at the beginning of every relationship whether or not they'd eventually want to commit to it. It's not something that dawns on them after months or years of auditions. So if you offer a man everything he wants without requiring a commitment *beforehand*, he will quite happily take the sex and carry on seeing you. Why wouldn't he? Why wouldn't anyone?

Combine this with the 'Don't frighten him off!' wisdom that we all hear now, where you're not allowed to mention any word that begins with 'M' for the first nine years in case he runs for the hills, and you've created a no-win situation. Men aren't talking about marriage, so women aren't either. Men are known to be commitmentphobes, so women pretend to be even bigger commitmentphobes. Men enjoy uncommitted sex, so heck, women will bloody well enjoy it too! Or at least we'll *say* that we do, so hopefully he'll go all clingy and be the one who's begging us to settle down.

Sometimes this works. If you can be *genuinely* uncommitted, there's a chance your man will be the one begging you to get married. But it's incredibly hard to be genuinely uncommitted if you're having sex with a man. I tried to play hard to get in a sexual relationship, and it was the most miserable experience of my life. Even Ellen Fein, co-author of *The Rules*, has admitted in interviews that she used to lie on her bed sobbing when playing hard-to-get with a man she really liked. It's nightmarish to have to *pretend* not to be mad about someone in case they get bored with you. Who wants to think about that possibility every day? Who wants to patrol their every action, guarding against accidentally letting slip with too much affection and seeing him start to yawn? Instead, it's far better to actually *be* uncommitted, by not having sex, and by seeing more than one man at a time.

We need to take charge of our own happiness, by making men work for the pleasure of having our company. When you see more than one man at a time, you are setting up the challenge. You aren't strapping yourself into a one-sided contract where you offer a man your body and your heart, and in return he gets to decide at his leisure whether or not he'll commit to you. You're moving back to the old-fashioned way of dating where the male is the one trying to encourage the female to commit.

Multiple-Dating Speeds up Commitment

Men realize that if you see other men, the other men may work a bit harder than they do, and therefore they are constantly faced with the possibility of losing you to someone else. This will make a lot of men raise their game and try to work harder to win you over. But it will make others drop out of the race early on.

That's a good thing! Don't take it to mean multiple dating will be a constant, tearful cycle of agonizing rejection. All I mean is, the men who can't give you what you want – safety and security – won't hang around for years like they do when you're bonking them.

And because there is always another man, or another date, you'll spend far less time obsessing over one person's actions. Nothing takes your mind off one man's disinterest than the adoring attentions of many others.

How to Multiple-Date

Step One: Meet Lots of Men

Obviously you can't see more than one man at once until you've got more than one man. But as most of us struggle to meet even one likely boyfriend candidate per *year*, this might seem like the hardest part of the entire process. And it will be, if you keep looking for likely boyfriend candidates. The thing to do is just look for lots of men.

At this point I know you're staring at the page in horror, imagining the long procession of uglies I'm going to convince you to date. I might even have been thrown into the corner of the room, where I'm now lecturing the skirting-board on how to meet new people.

Relax, would you? I'm not going to be encouraging you to hook-up with the homeless or start writing to men on Death Row. But you're only allowed to set a few basic requirements, and *any* man who fulfils them should be classed as dateable in your eyes.

Why? Because it stops you only going for men you consider 'your type' and starts letting you experience lots of different types of men. Instead of getting into the same relationship over and over, which is what most of us do, you'll be opening yourself up to new personalities. Very few of us end up with the man we always imagined.

Get out the Cosmic Shopping List I encouraged you to write in Chapter Two. (You did do this, didn't you? You must have known I'd be testing you on stuff like this.) If you did it, pick three things from the list that are your total non-negotiables. These aren't shallow traits like 'Great sense of humour!' or 'Hung like a baboon'. They're practical things like age, status (i.e. divorced or single), height, children or no children, and so on.

If you didn't do the List before, do it now. Write down three things you *need* in a man. Not things that you want, but things you need him to have, or be, or do. In case you're wondering, 'Owns a Ferrari' is a want; 'Owns a car' is a need. 'Prefers women with really big bums' is a want; 'Prefers women' is a need.

Now you've done your non-negotiables, they're the only vetting you're allowed to do when you meet a man. As long as he meets those three minimum requirements, you *have* to go out with him if he asks. You don't have to marry him, but you have to see him. And more than once, unless he treats you badly or is so boring you start hacking at your wrists with the butter-knife during dinner.

Once you've lowered your screening process in this way, you'll start to realize that there are more men in the world than you ever imagined. Instead of ignoring men who don't look like your last six exes, you'll start noticing the men who are interested in you.

Remember, you're not going to be sleeping with any of

these men. You're just going to be open to dating them for a while. That's all. Look, if the worst comes to the worst, you'll get some free dinners out of the process and a chance to practise new clothing combinations. And you'll get loads of dating practice which you'd never have got if you limited yourself to dating only men you think might be *Him*.

But I Never Meet Anyone

Yes, you do, and now you'll see that you do. Instead of only noticing the men you fancy, you'll start noticing the men who fancy you, too. That tiny guy in the corner of the restaurant who requested a booster-seat just so he could catch your eye – unless height was on your List, he is a candidate for dating. The man in the next office who smiles at you every morning – before, you'd have let those hairy arms put you off, but now if he asks you out, you're going to go. Think of it as frog-kissing. Think of it as a numbers game. Or don't think about it at all, just promise yourself that, for now, Anyone Goes.

Where to Meet Men

Here's that old Agony-Aunt favourite: 'Join a new club! Take up a new hobby!' I'd recommend dance classes like Salsa where you get to ram yourself up against available men, or cookery classes since men decided that being a chef is sexy. My friend Anita had great luck taking motorcycle maintenance classes, which were deluged with biker boys, but it helped that she actually owned her own bike and didn't mind men taking their engines apart on her sofa.

If you want to meet the most amount of men in the shortest time, become a Prison Warden. Or try Internet Dating.

Tips for Internet Dating

I met my husband on Match.com, and I'm now their Relationship Expert, so I feel smugly satisfied enough to give you tips here.

- Date safely.

    Always meet online suitors in a public place, tell other people where you're going, and never leave drinks unattended.

- Don't limit yourself to one dating website, get your profile up on several.

    If your List has Minimum Requirements like 'Must have a PhD' or 'Earns more than £50K a year', you can choose websites that cater for brainiacs and high-achievers. But don't limit yourself to niche websites – put your advert on the larger sites too, just to increase your chances of being seen.

- Agonize more over your photo than your profile.

    Men are visual creatures. Don't throw on a so-so picture then spend all night composing a lyrical profile, because men won't even bother to read your words if they don't find you attractive.

    Spend an evening getting glammed up and have a

friend take loads of pictures of you on a digital camera (so you can delete icky ones quicker, and upload nice ones immediately). Choose a head shot and a full-length shot that shows your figure. Don't worry if you use a photo that shows you looking unusually good, unless you have changed drastically since it was taken, like gaining twenty stone or twenty years. It's better to get a great photo up and get dates coming in, because that'll increase your chances of actually meeting someone who might fall for your personality in real life.

- Write a 'feminine' profile.

Don't boast about your great salary or go too over-board with your career triumphs. The right man will admire your career success but it won't be what attracted him to you. Instead, write a profile that describes you as a *woman*. Men are looking for women, not other men, so play up your sensual side. What you like to eat, where you like travelling to, films you love watching, what makes you laugh. Don't make it too long, either. Remember he gets to find out about you when he actually takes you out for a date.

- Issue a challenge.

My friend Caroline was just starting golf lessons when she wrote her Udate profile, so she included the line, 'Preference will be given to men who can help me with my golf swing.' Many men wrote back giving her tips and offering to take her out for a game. Her future husband wrote to her apologizing that he couldn't play golf, but listed the sports he *could* help her with.

- Don't be negative.

   You'd be surprised how many online daters advertise the fact that they've been unlucky in love. Since when was this a sexy quality? 'Users and players need not apply,' 'My heart is a peach which bruises easily,' 'Looking to trust again,' are all lines I've read on dating sites, and which are about as off-putting as writing, in capitals, 'LOVERS WERE ALWAYS WALKING OUT ON ME UNTIL I STARTED KEEPING THEM IN MY CELLAR.' Keep it very light. Don't you dare write anything about any relationship you've had before. If you are prone to spilling your guts, remember that people you know – work colleagues, exes, your younger brother – might stumble across your advert, so keep it brief and not incriminating.

- Don't spend your life emailing.

   If you're like me, you'll fall in love with someone's emails and create this adorable fantasy man in your imagination, which will then be tragically crushed when you finally meet, in person, the most hideous man you've ever seen. So cut to the chase and meet up soon. The first few emails should be brief and chatty, and if he doesn't suggest meeting up within the first three emails, stop writing back. That'll either encourage him to ask for your phone number, or stop you emailing forever with a man who doesn't want to meet you, just wants to have loads of pen pals. (There are more of these than you'd think. And they're usually already in relationships.)

Another way to encourage a man towards meeting you is to email him your phone number. If you're nervous about giving it out to strangers, sign up for a 'Follow Me' number. That's a number you rent (it's just a few pounds a year) which you can give out to online men. When they dial it, the call is automatically diverted to your mobile number, or home number. It saves you giving out your real numbers to anyone you don't know for sure isn't gibbering in their shed, carving your effigy out of soap. Try *www.telecomsworldplc.co.uk*, or *www.iccommunications.co.uk* for more details and to sign up.

Step Two: Build up a Rotation

A 'rotation' is literally a group of men that you're dating. You'll have men in there that you like more than others, but you should treat them all equally. The point is to go out with all of them and watch to see who you like best, and who treats you the nicest. Remember, your goal is to let the best man win you. It might not be the man you are most attracted to on the first date – in fact, it's usually not.

Bryony, 31, used multiple-dating as a way to ease herself back into the dating scene after a failed long-term, live-in relationship.

I had just moved out of a six-year live-in relationship and knew that I had no more time to waste finding Mr Right. It had taken me almost two years of on-again, off-again with my ex before I finally ended things, so I was twenty-nine and ready to settle down.

The first thing I did was make sure my life was in order. I wanted to attract a man who was 'sorted', so I knew I had to be in a good place with my finances, my health, my job, my looks and my confidence. I took overtime at work and paid off my loans, then started a gym membership to get fitter and healthier. Next up, I put online dating adverts up on Match, Lava Life and Love@Lycos, then I accepted dates with everyone who asked me. Often they were just initial coffee-dates to see if there was any chemistry first. But I didn't rule out any men – if they were halfway decent, I saw them again. I knew that the more men I dated, the more 'out there' I'd feel, and the more confidence I'd gain.

I had already met two likely prospects online when I received a sweet email from a lawyer called Mark. He asked for my phone number and I gave it to him, despite being more interested in Richard, a sexy actor I was seeing from Match. Mark rang me early the following week to set up a dinner date, and I agreed.

Meanwhile, Richard was starting to push me for sex. We'd had a good few snogging sessions when I told him I wasn't looking to get too hot and heavy right away. He left my flat in a bit of a huff and I worried that I'd annoyed him. Usually I'd have stayed home to mope, but the next night I had a date with Mark.

Mark took me to a lovely restaurant and, despite my being keen on Richard, I noticed that Mark was very attentive and sweet. He made sure my glass of wine was never empty and asked me lots of questions. It was an easy, fun first date.

The next week Richard rang me and I was delighted. He asked me out for Friday night, but I had to say no because Mark had already booked me to go to the cinema. Richard sounded suitably curious when I said I already had plans with 'friends' and suggested Saturday instead. I was still thinking about that when Friday came and Mark took me to see a lovely film and brought me a bunch of flowers. I thought that was a bit mushy, but when Richard arrived on Saturday empty-handed it felt good to see him looking at the flowers.

Over the next couple of weeks, I still accepted more dates from Match, but noticed that Mark had taken his advert down. I didn't mention it until Mark asked me if I was seeing anyone else. I told him, 'I'm accepting dates from other men, but nothing serious. I don't want to get into anything too heavy just for now.' He said he understood, and that as soon as I was looking for more I should let him know. Then he asked me out for the following week.

Richard finally vanished after our sixth sex-free date and I was feeling low, but Mark was always there to cheer me up with a sweet date suggestion. Finally, after a lovely dinner, Mark asked again if I could see him 'exclusively' and I agreed. He looked so chuffed, like he'd won the lottery! A week later we slept together and it felt lovely to be with a man who adored me. We got married a year later.

Yes, I know. Happiness is annoying and Bryony's fairytale ending could almost make you feel a bit unhinged, like you'd be tempted to chat up her husband at parties to see if he really *is* that devoted. Er, you know, if you were a bit unstable. Of course, I'd never do anything like that, and I know you wouldn't either.

Anyway, the beauty of multiple-dating is that it's comparison shopping. It allows you to experience different men simultaneously, and stops you taking any one of them too seriously. Monday night you might meet Simon for a drink in the pub, and fall madly in love as he talks to you about growing his own vegetables on an allotment. But then on Tuesday, you see Steve, and realize that a City banker is more your scene, as he wines and dines you at the Oxo Tower. He wants to see you again the next evening, but you can't – you're already seeing Stuart, who wrote to you on Match.com and fancies a night at the cinema. Thursday night you stay in to alphabetize your underwear, then Friday you go out with the girls and meet Scott, who asks you out for lunch the next day . . .

Remember, you're not madly in love with any of these men, you're just accepting dates from men who approach you, and adopting a mature 'wait and see' approach. Meanwhile, they are all being driven nuts by your busy schedule and all the bouquets of flowers that magically appear in your flat.

Keep the Rotation Going Until You Have a Winner

Soon it'll be clear to you that you like one of your dates more than the others. You'll feel sure that that's a sign to stop multiple-dating and concentrate on Mr Wonderful. Is it? No. Usually, it's a sign that you should keep on doing what you're doing.

Don't drop any men in your Rotation unless they treat you badly or make you miserable. Some will stop dating you naturally anyway, after two or three dates with no nookie. That's a good thing to happen, so don't let yourself get too upset over it. Badmouth them on dating blogs on the Internet, obviously, and send their email address to known spam-sites, but don't mope around sobbing for a month. Those men were only around for what they could get and realized that they didn't have what it took to get into a commitment with you. Better after two or three dates than two or three years.

The only reason to stop dating your Rotation is when one of the men is so taken with you that he starts booking up all of your time. He'll start asking you out for every Saturday night so you can't go out and meet anyone else. He'll start asking you way in advance for dates on New Year's Eve, your birthday, Christmas ... You'll begin feeling that you don't have time to see anyone else, because one bloke is just always *there*.

Even then, don't rush into cancelling all your other dates. Give it another week or so until you feel sure you want to enter into an exclusive relationship with him, and that you're well on the way to commitment.

Should I Tell Him I'm Multiple-Dating?

Love means never having to say, 'You're my eighteenth date this week!' So, no, you don't have to spell it out. If you're taking things slowly as advised in Chapter Two – not indulging in hang-out dates, only kissing him and not grinding against him like a spaniel against the arm of the sofa – then really the relationship won't be at a stage when you have to start divulging what you're doing every night you're not seeing him. It'll be light and friendly, not intense and soul-baring.

I was just doing some research among my male friends, and was surprised to discover that many men actually assume you're seeing other people at the beginning of relationships. The worst 'player' among the males I questioned said, 'There's always someone else on the scene when you first meet a girl. Someone she's sleeping with occasionally, an ex she's still in touch with, someone she fancies at work ... I wouldn't ask her about the men in her life until we'd slept together. It's not really my business until then.'

If you're the type who feels guilty about accepting dates from more men when you're starting to date someone, you could be completely honest and tell everyone, 'I want you to know I'm interested in taking things slowly for a while, and just seeing what happens. I'm not looking to jump headlong into a relationship right this minute.' He'll know what this means. And it will have the benefit of kick-starting his interest, if he's keen on you.

When I was living in a flat in London, around the time I met my husband, an American girl called Sam moved into the flat opposite mine. We used to get together for coffee every week or so, and she told me how she'd started seeing two men. One was an exotic music producer whom she had a raging crush on, and the other was a sweetheart called Ben. Sam was so keen on the music producer, she never had the courage to admit to him that there was someone else on the scene, but she did tell Ben.

After a month or so, it was clear that Ben was going to be the winner. He was just always there. He'd come to her flat to fix things, take her out on romantic walks, turn up with little presents. From being the second-favourite in the race when it started, he pulled straight into the lead. He never let the thought of another man put him off. It only made him more determined to prove himself. They're married now, with a child.

Use Men's Competitive Nature to Your Advantage

If you've ever had a man pursue you when you've had a boyfriend, you'll know first-hand how there is nothing more likely to perk up a man's interest. All the men I've asked about multiple-dating said the same thing: 'If I thought a girl was going on dates with other men while she was seeing me, it would make me more interested, if I liked her. It would be a challenge.'

But the point of doing this isn't to play a load of men off against one another in order to get more dates, dinners and diamonds. Karmically that won't work, they'll all chuck you simultaneously, you'll die alone and no-one will come to your funeral. The idea is to use the fact that you are being pursued by several different suitors to keep yourself more calm and centred while you find the man that's *right* for you.

And success breeds success. We've all experienced the phenomenon where nobody looks at us for five years until we finally start dating someone, then men magically appear in our lives and start asking us out. Multiple-dating makes every day like that.

Questions

How long are you advising I multiple-date for? I can't imagine I could do this for more than a few weeks.

A few weeks is fine. Really, there's no way to know before you get out there and start doing it. Some men will drop off the face of the earth within two or three dates anyway, so you won't have to worry about them. But the good thing about multiple-dating is, you're not suddenly left with zero prospects when one man ditches you. You have other men still on the scene.

I still can't believe you're telling me to go out with anyone. I just can't enjoy myself on a date if there's no sexual chemistry. What's the point?

I know what you mean, and I'm not telling you to deliberately seek out men who are so revolting, you'll be the cheapest dinner-date in history because you can barely eat in front of them. What I'm saying is, don't reject men *purely* on the basis that you can't immediately see yourself marrying them. Often the men that are the worst for us are the ones we have an immediate chemistry with. They're the ones who cause us to go bonkers and lose ourselves, because that attraction means it's really hard to judge whether or not they're actually *good* for us. We just know that we want them, not that they are necessarily treating us nicely or making us happy.

When you start accepting dates from less immediately sexy suitors, you're opening yourself up to having calmer, more steady relationships. You can keep a clearer head.

What if one of my dates sees me out with someone else? Won't he hate me?

This is where it pays to remind you that multiple-dating is something you can only do if you're not sleeping with anyone. If you are always chaste and restrained on your dates with Jim, he will assume that you're being equally chaste and restrained with Ben, if he catches you together. Besides, he can't get angry with you because you haven't led him on or lied to him – it's early days, he knows he can't expect you to stay at home cross-stitching your veil on the nights he's not around. What will probably happen is that Jim will suddenly realize that other men are still asking you out, and that he had better pull out all the stops to get you interested in him. If he doesn't, he wasn't that bothered. And a lot of the point of doing multiple-dating (and not having casual sex) is that you don't waste loads of time on men who aren't bothered.

If one of my dates sends me flowers, should I hide them before another date comes round to my house?

Not unless he has chronic hay-fever. No, don't hide your flowers, or invitations or presents or anything another man gave you (except maybe love-bites). Don't rub them in his *face*, but don't feel the need to shove them in the freezer when your doorbell rings. A man knows that you are effectively still 'on the market' before he's taken you off it (by proposing), so seeing flowers from other men will remind him that you're still in demand. Besides, men often value something purely because it is prized by someone else.

Questions to Say 'Yes' to Before You Say 'Yes' to Him

I can't just be with someone just because it's great sex. Orgasms don't last long enough.

Courteney Cox

Will tonight ever be The Night? Yes, of course. If you've decided to wait until engagement or marriage, you'll know exactly when the Big Night will happen. If you're waiting till engagement, he'll drop to one knee and you won't let him get up again; or if you're waiting till marriage, you simply Don't until you've said 'I do'.

But what if you're just waiting for him to be truly smitten with you? Before you hop into bed, here are some questions to answer before you drag him up the stairs. They take into account his feelings, your feelings, the state of your relationship and how likely it is that this is the right man *and* the right time.

Before you say 'Yes' to him, make sure you can say 'Yes' to

all these questions first. If you can't, wait a few more dates, a few more weeks or a few more boyfriends. I know you're sorely tempted, but it'll be worth it. Remember, prude is short for prudent.

Are You by Yourself at this Moment?

Obviously, the right time to decide if you're ready to have sex with a new man is when you're on your own and still capable of rational thought, but how many of us actually do that? Most of us are still weighing up whether or not to bonk him when he's already underneath the duvet and making determined headway in a southerly direction. Therefore, the decision about one of the most important turning points in a relationship usually goes like this: 'It's still too soon for us to have sex because . . . ooh, that's nice . . . nope, concentrate, yes, we can't bonk yet because I still don't know whether he liiiikes meeeee . . . Where did he learn to do that? . . . Jesus . . . where was I? Yes, I'm still not sure if we are on the same page about marriage . . . oh my God, that's good . . . I thought he said he was vegetarian? Oh help, that's lovely . . . Oh yes . . . quickly, the reasons we shouldn't have sex are . . . are . . . are . . . aaaah.'

And then the decision has been made for you. I don't want you to do that this time, though. I want you to be as coolly calculating as Robocop, because sex is one of the biggest decisions you'll make in a relationship. Don't cross your fingers and hope that he turns out to be one of the good guys – cross your legs and make rational choices before he starts trying to undo your self-control and your bra.

The truth is, one night either way won't make much difference, so you can always say, 'Not yet'. It doesn't feel like it when you really adore a man. When you've had a perfect date, and you're walking hand-in-hand along the riverbank gazing at the stars together, it seems like having an awesome rogering would be the icing on the cake. Or you feel it's the least you could do, really, seeing how he paid for the meal and was really understanding when you knocked your wine over. But don't act on the spur of the moment. Promise me? You can't un-bonk a man, but you can always bonk him tomorrow night . . . if the answers to the remaining questions are 'Yes'.

Are You Sober?

I'm just asking! No need to get angry and throw your gin in my face. It's just that we don't want you to be making any major decisions based on the knicker-elastic-loosening effects of booze. Alcohol is terrible for two reasons. 1: it lowers your inhibitions; and 2: it makes people appear better-looking than they really are. So don't drink and grind. Instead, try to get through a date without touching booze at all, and see if he is still as funny, sexy and smart then. (Or if, indeed, you are.) If he is, and all the other questions here get a 'Yes', then shag away!

Are You in Love With Him?

Call me an old romantic fool, call me a wet blanket, but don't call any man you're not in love with to offer him a night of violent romping. Why not? Apart from the fact that it's a waste of your time, it might also affect your very-long-term happiness. Remember oxytocin? The bonding hormone? When we have sex, we release lots of it – especially if we orgasm. But if we have *uncommitted* sex, we also release opiate-like endorphins. These soothe the stress we feel when we have sex (an act that makes us vulnerable) with someone we don't trust. Over time, these opiates will limit the amount of oxytocin we produce, making us much more likely to have issues with bonding, commitment and being able to have a successful marriage. The abstinence-promoters in America cite this as *the* most important reason not to have premarital sex.

As you know, I don't believe that sex should necessarily be saved for marriage, for the simple reason that it might make you marry a man out of lust and not love. But I do think that sex is too powerful to our happiness to be given away like out-of-date milk.

Does He Fix Your Stuff?

This question is to ascertain if he really loves you, or just really wants the pair of you to take your clothes off and get all sweaty together.

Men who are in love with you fix your stuff. They want to be useful to you, to serve a purpose. The most common way they show this is by strapping on a tool belt and giving up their time to do manly jobs around your place. If the only place your partner does manly jobs is in the loo, don't have sex with him.

Of course, your man might be hopeless at DIY, but you still want to see solid evidence – again, not just in the U-bend – that he will *give up his time* to make your life better. So he might help you buy a new car by actively taking you to dealerships, researching models in *AutoTrader*, and inspecting the bodywork of cars you're thinking of buying. Needless to say, all the time he's doing any of this he isn't huffing and puffing and making you feel bad about it. He should be helping you willingly. You should find yourself saying things like, 'Are you sure you don't mind taking me to Edinburgh? You're so good to me!' not mumbling apologies and promising you'll make it up to him somehow.

He should also be showing concern for your well-being. Men who love you feel protective – think of your Dad waiting outside school discos to pick you up at midnight – so he'll be great about giving you lifts home at night, and calling to see how you got on at the doctor's. And he'll just *be there* a lot. If you don't see or hear from him very often, don't shag him to try to bring him closer. He'll feel closer in the literal, proximity sense, but he won't be any closer emotionally. Let your heart grow cold towards any man who isn't around enough to warm it up.

Does Your Work Receptionist Recognize His Voice?

Or your flatmate? Or your colleagues? Or your pets? A man who loves you – and isn't at risk of drifting away after nookie faster than the smoke from your post-coital cigarette – tries to make himself known to people in your life. He'll call you a *lot*, and be nice to anyone who answers the phone. He'll also be adorable to your friends and your family, and even your pets. The reason for this is simple: he knows these people have influence in your life and he doesn't want anyone to talk you out of dating him.

There are also other, more insecure reasons for his attentiveness – if he loves you he is scared of losing you. Oscar Wilde said, 'The essence of romance is uncertainty.' He doesn't feel safe and relaxed; he feels a slight undercurrent of abject terror. Why? Because love makes us idolize our partner. Even though the rest of the world might look at you and wish you'd sew up the holes in your balaclava, he will think you are beautiful. (Remember the limerance.) So, to increase his chances of keeping you, he will suck up to people in your life so they'll say things to you like, 'You can't chuck him! He's adorable!'

A man who thinks more of himself than you won't bother to ingratiate himself. He'll be more concerned with what he thinks about your friends than what they think about him. Long term, this is a bad sign. So don't risk kicking off your bonding response, hold back until you have proof that he adores you.

Have You Got a Key to His House?

And not just one that he gave you so you could go round and clean. A man who adores you will be like an open book, he'll welcome you into his life and *want you near him a lot*. To make this happen, he'll offer you a key so you can come and go as you like. He'll point out that his place has a better shower than yours, so you could use it after the gym. He'll mention that he has every single episode of *Coupling* on DVD. He'll get all mushy and tell you that he fantasizes about coming home from work and finding you there.

His giving you a key – willingly, not after you've worn him down about it, or threatened him with a bar of soap and said you'd make your own – is a brilliant sign of his commitment. It means he has nothing to hide. He has burned his exes' photographs and deleted all their emails from his computer (if he has any sense, with you about to roam around there like a forensics specialist). You should expect nothing less from a man before you let him put his Yale in your lock.

Of course, you shouldn't accept his key for the first four or five months of dating, so that's another reason it's on this list. I don't want you collecting men's keys so you can walk around swinging a massive bunch of them, like a security guard. You should only accept the key to a man's flat when you are sure that you're going to probably make a Go of Things.

Have You Met his Friends a Couple of Times?

Beware the boyfriend who only ever takes you along to dates with other people – like parties or drinks with his mates. Men who are in love with you want to spend their time with just you, free from any onlookers. In this way they are very similar to men who think you're ugly.

The perfect man will take you along to occasional group outings so he can show you off to all of his friends, but want plenty of nights out with you alone, too. (Notice I said nights *out* – a once-a-week wrestling match on his sofa isn't a sign of much more than the fact that he's still hoping against hope that you might give up all this silly 'waiting' nonsense.)

A man who sees you only as a Booty Call, or a Good-For-Now girl, will either dilute your company (until bedtime) with other people, or he'll only see you by yourself and *never* with his friends.

It's also significant if he's introduced you to his family. It's not vital – in fact, some men introduce everyone to their family, regardless of whether they like them or not. (This is obviously a moot point if he still lives at home.) I still think the friends test is much more significant. Let's face it, it's much scarier to show your friends who you're dating, because you know they'll be much more critical than any member of your family (except sisters). But one minger and your mates will never let you live it down.

Have You Both Had AIDS Tests?

This is important not just because of all that stuff about health risks, infection, death, blah blah blah. AIDS tests tell you more than whether one of you is HIV Positive – they tell you how serious you are about each other. Let's face it, nobody wants to be the killjoy with a clipboard, asking lovers to list the names and addresses of everyone they've ever bonked. And for most casual affairs you wouldn't do that – but you would use condoms. With this new kind of dating, I want you to be able to talk about the big issues BEFORE you bonk. Because it shows you are comfortable enough with one other to do so.

Most couples today fall into bed then fall into the

relationship that comes afterwards. This easy-come, easy-come method of dating requires you to *not* talk about important issues, like AIDS or marriage or children, because that would put the other person off. These days we have to be light and breezy, because sex makes everything we say carry more weight.

But when you're not having sex, you can talk about Big Things. It's more intimate when you're not spending most evenings wiping bodily fluids off one another. You don't have to worry about scaring the other person away, because you've already done the scariest thing you could – withhold sex. Any man who sticks with you through months of no nookie is in it for the long haul. He likes you for *you*, and therefore of course he'll be happy to take an AIDS test if that makes you happy. He cares about your health. He'll do whatever it takes.

And besides, it takes a couple of weeks for the results to come back.

Is This Your Idea?

Pressure can be the reason why loads of us end up in bed. I don't necessarily mean pressure from our boyfriend, either.

Friends can sabotage our abstinence pledge in a million ways. For example, have you ever tried to go on a diet and then found that your girlfriends are sweet but hopeless – suggesting you all meet at Pizza Hut, buying you a box of chocolates when you lose half a pound, or encouraging you to knock back one more glass of wine when you have told them a million times (because you're drunk) that it contains 200 calories?

Well, those same adorable but unhelpful friends can also encourage you to go to bed with your bloke before you're 100 per cent certain.

I don't mean to suggest they're trying to undermine you, because nine times out of ten, if you have lovely friends, that won't be the case. I don't even mean to suggest that your friends are making bad life judgements for themselves and want to drag you down with them into trollopy Hell. I just mean, firstly, that friends usually suggest what they think will make you happy. They don't want to be Debbie Downers, telling you not to have premarital sex because it is against the Holy Code of chastity, when saying, 'Yeah! Shag him! I have and it was great!' will make you laugh.

But secondly, as Erica Jong said, '. . . advice is what we ask for when we know what to do but wish we didn't.' If you're asking your girlfriends if they think you could get away with shagging your boyfriend now, the chances are that you don't think you can, but you thought you'd ask them so they could talk you into it. If you knew it was the wrong time to shag, or the absolute right time to shag, you wouldn't ask them. It's when you're in that middle stage that you find yourself handing out questionnaires.

So don't trust your friends to tell you the right thing to do.

With tactical chastity, it's usually okay, because most

women will understand why you're doing this. Let's face it, who among us hasn't been hurt by a man after bonking him too soon? But when you start to ask around for advice, they'll tell you what you want to hear.

Another person likely to be putting the, er, screws on you is a man who isn't in love. Men in love are pushovers, and will encourage you to do whatever makes you happy. A man not in love will encourage you to do whatever makes him happy. The pressure can come directly – 'I don't think I can handle a sex-free relationship' – or indirectly – 'This makes me think you don't know how much I care for you, and that makes me question Us' – but either way you'll feel a bit unsure after the conversation. *That's* the only thing to listen to – the voice in your head that says, 'Something about this feels wrong.'

Do You Talk About the Future?

And by this I mean your joint future, not both of you trading your personal ambitions like little kids. 'When I grow up I'm going to be an astronaut.' 'Well, I'm going to be an air stewardess!' This is another tip that goes against current dating wisdom, which says that you should never mention the future to a man, because it will send him running into the nearest monastery so fast his feet will catch fire.

Well, I agree that you shouldn't be the one to bring up your future, but if he's keen to talk about it, I say go for it. You're not having sex with him, so many things in dating will happen faster than they would normally. Sex slows down a man's pursuit. It satisfies him and makes him happy in the here and now. Then suddenly you wake up five years later and realize you're still in the still-here and now-what?

In contrast, a man not having sex with you will think about your shared future very quickly. (Mainly because that's where all the nookie is.) He'll know early on if he wants to marry you, or have a long-term relationship, and he'll be eager to share it because he wants you to know he's serious about you. He'll talk about weddings and kids, holidays and pension plans, retirement, everything, and it'll be clear that he sees you in that future with him.

This is not enough on its own, of course, to judge how serious a man is. Loads of men will attempt to sucker you in with future-talk to make you think he sees you as a long-term bet. He'll be worse than Nostradamus. But when combined with everything else on this list, it'll give you a good idea that he's serious.

Do You Know You're not Going to Get Pregnant?

Good. Carry on then. Just checking.

Have You Been Dating Him for at Least Six Months?

At the beginning, men who just want a bunk-up act the same as men who want to marry you, which is why I urge you to wait as long as you can. Don't be afraid to let a man get bored and disappear. This process is about weeding out the so-so suitors and getting past them quickly so you can meet the men who are besotted by you. You have to kiss a lot of frogs to meet your prince. Just be relieved you don't have to shag them.

Are You Happy to Wait a Bit Longer?

The best time to have first-time sex isn't when you are over-come with lust, feeling that if he doesn't rip off his anorak *this very minute* you'll die. I know it feels like that, but uh-uh. That's an impulse decision and impulse decisions are usually fuelled by a need for something else. Like when you go shopping. Sometimes the clothes you blew your overdraft on end up being the much-loved staples that you love and wear every day. But more often, they end up in the back of your wardrobe unworn. They weren't what you actually really wanted. You probably just felt depressed or unloved or pre-menstrual. Which is one thing when you're only talking about a scarf, but quite another when it's the wrong man you have hanging round your neck.

Instead, the best time for bonkage is when you probably could wait another few months, but you're so happy and secure that you don't *need* to. And he should feel the same way. Not after an argument when you feel you want to get close to each other again. Not when one of you is going away for a while. But when you're both feeling calm and centred.

Now You Can Ask Me Questions

I can answer 'Yes' to all these questions, except we've only been dating for three months. Surely I don't need to keep waiting?

It would be better if you did. This is not the time to 'pull him back in' with sex. Yes, it'll keep him around a bit longer, but it won't have an impact on his emotions. You don't want someone who's only around for nookie. If you can say 'Yes' to all the other questions, he doesn't sound uncommitted so you're probably with a genuinely keen man. In which case, why will it hurt to wait another few dates?

Nobody who tries abstinence ever regrets waiting. Ask any couple you know – they will never say that they wished they'd had sex earlier in the relationship. But you'll know plenty of girls who woke up the next morning after impulsive nookie and thought, 'Oops.'

♥

He's getting angry with me. This isn't working.

Yes, it *is* working! You're getting to see the real him, which is someone who's used to getting his own way. It's natural for him to feel grumpy when his lover isn't performing like all the others did. But did he marry any of the others? Hmmm?

Grumpiness, though, is a sign that he's putting what he wants above what you want. If he was scared of losing you, he'd feel grumpy in private but at least *pretend* to be okay with waiting when he's in your company. He'd cross his legs to cover his steaming erection and say that the pain in his testicles will soon go away. He wouldn't dare express negative emotions around you in case you told him to kindly bugger off. So that's not a good omen. You can still give him a few more dates, though, and see what he does. If he carries on making you feel guilty, chuck him.

♥

It's so hard to tell him to stop when it feels so right.

Uh oh. You're at the 'everything but' stage, aren't you? Yes, I agree, this bit is agony. Pull back a bit so you're having more outside dates again, and fewer make-out sessions on the sofa. Sometimes the only thing that can stop us shagging is knowing that everyone else in the cinema can hear us.

♥

He's told his friends – they think I'm weird.

Hold on, he told his friends, and then he told *you* he told his friends? This I don't like. Not the fact that he told his mates, but that he's using this to put indirect pressure on you about your decision. This is passive-aggression. Men like this are a headache. 'I'm fine with waiting, but Andy thinks you must have been hurt before.' Oh, sod off you big moaner. If he does this again, stop the date right then, at that very minute, and say you want to go home. Don't say why, just that you think you're going to go home now. Then leave him to stew for twenty-four hours before you talk to him again. By pulling back immediately, you're saying that you won't put up with it. It will frighten him and make him do a complete turnaround. Oh, and find out Andy's home address. You might have been hurt before but it's nothing compared to what Andy's got coming.

♥

His ex is sniffing around – how can I compete with a girl he's already slept with?

There's no comparison. To understand this, you have to learn to think like a man. For men, novelty is one of the strongest parts of the sex drive. Every woman that he hasn't had is more exciting than anyone he's had every which way. You are still uncharted territory, an unread book, a mystery. He will never feel he has you until, well, he's had you. The ex, by comparison, is old news. He looks at her and knows what she looks like in bed. He knows how she feels, tastes and sounds. She'll never be the one that got away.

If he goes back to her, he was either never that keen on you, or was still keen on her.

♥

He's pressuring me.

Don't see him for a couple of weeks. He's got too confident.

♥

He's NOT pressuring me!

Firstly, it might be a good idea to check that both of his testicles are still in place and functional. If they are, just carry on doing what you're not doing.

If you need inspiration, watch old black and white films where the heroine engages in a battle of wits with a suitor. (*Indiscreet* with Cary Grant and Ingrid Bergman is perfect for this.) You'll see how it can often take everything the woman has to hold back her boiling frustration while keeping an aloof demeanour. You're not alone! Hang in there – he won't hold out on you forever. Just work through the other stages – future talk, meeting his friends, all that – and when he finally breaks, you'll be all set to jump aboard.

Afterglow or Afterburn?

> *The problem is that God gives men a brain and a penis,*
> *and only enough blood to run one at a time.*
>
> Robin Williams

So You've Shagged Him . . .

Congratulations! How was it? Was it, you know . . .? Oh God, sorry. Of course you're not going to answer personal questions like that out loud reading a book. That would be no use at all. Please send all salacious details to me in an email, care of my publisher.

And how do you feel now? Hopefully you feel fabulous. Hopefully you waited till the right time in your relationship – until it was committed, secure and exclusive, and everything was wonderful. So now, post-bonk, everything should look rosy. (Although hopefully not your genitals, because that could signal an infection.)

Of course you waited until the time was perfect and so you feel fine. But for others reading this who maybe didn't display your immense self-control and sassiness, we could use this chapter to discuss, you know, what to do if, say, ooh, some random girl didn't actually wait that long, but in fact jumped, well, pretty much into bed with her boyfriend a few dates after meeting him.

So Now What?

Keep Your Own Life

Starting from the morning after the night before, force yourself to focus on all the fun things you have going on in your life. I don't know why this is so hard sometimes, but it can be, especially after that First Bonk. I know you might want to do everything together from now on, but please remember to pace the relationship, *especially* if you like him.

Get out of bed first, and force yourself not to leap back in for some more 'cuddle time' by consciously and deliberately focussing on something fun that you have planned to do later in the day. Make it something that he's not involved in: getting your boobs measured, say, or a gossipy lunch with your girlfriends. Always have somewhere else to go and something else to do. This makes you more attractive – not least to yourself.

Don't Immediately Assume That the Sex Means You Can Open Up About Everything

One of the most dangerous parts of too-soon sex is the false feeling of intimacy it creates. It's misleading. This is why people suggest you wait a while before dropping your thong. (We're not just trying to ruin your day, although of course that's a big part of it.) Relationships should be a slow, steady build-up of experiences. There should be a slow revealing of each other, like courses in a meal, movements in a symphony, stanzas in a poem ... oh, look, you've shagged. Quick! Now you feel really close to each other, tell him your credit-reference problems, your pending unemployment, your struggle with dandruff. It doesn't matter – you've had *sex* now. You're obviously really close to each other, he can take it! Confess all! Let it all out!

Do you see what I'm getting at? That afterglow makes you feel like you're in a lot deeper than you *actually* are. So try to take the sex lightly, once you've had it. Don't use it as an excuse to tell him everything about yourself. I know it's tempting, especially as you lay snuggled across his chest, his underpants still steaming damply across your bedside lamp, but you'll regret it as soon as you're away from him again. Even if he suddenly explodes in a volcano of confession, hold back. There's still a lot of getting-to-know you both need to do with each other, and the more you expose now, the less intrigued by you he'll be.

Yes, you can compliment him on the sex if it was amazing. But don't gush on and on like a geiser, saying it's the best sex you've ever had 'and I've had loads!' or anything that sounds vulnerable or needy.

Don't Feel That Every Date Now Has to Be a Sex Date

Every so often, go out for dinner and then kiss your boyfriend chastely goodnight at the door. If he looks surprised, say you've got a busy day planned for tomorrow, and that you need to sleep. He'll go through an elaborate mime-routine now, including puppy-dog eyes, pouty lip, trying to seduce you on your doorstep and then maybe a dramatic sulk and an angry stomp down the stairs. Don't you worry about it. He'll be back, keener than ever.

The reason for doing this is to keep the relationship from falling into a predictable routine where you find yourself having sex at the end of every date. Sex is not an after-dinner mint. That's way too comfortable a pattern to get into, especially if (like most of us) you have your sights set on settling down and getting married. Even if you're not marriage-minded, it's a good thing to keep a man on his toes, and off his elbows, now and then.

It's easiest to do this if you start early on. If you have sex on every date after the first Sex Date, he'll start to expect it and you'll then feel a bit weird about slamming the door on his stiffy. He'll be wondering if he's done something wrong, and you'll feel you need to supply doctor's notes just to get a night off.

Take Regular Holidays

And not with him. Repeat: not with him. Men fall in love with us in the times they don't see us, when they're missing us like mad and dying for us to be there. When my best friend had been dating her now-husband for three months, she booked a long weekend at a beauty-spa with a girlfriend. The next time she saw him he, totally unprompted, gave her a set of keys to his flat.

Be the busy girl who has loads of things to do. Airports are sexy. His calling your phone to hear it ring in that long international '*riiiiing*' instead of the boring '*ring ring*', is sexy. His not being able to get hold of you for two weeks is sexier still. And don't check in with him all the time during the holiday. If he insists, call him once when you get there to say your plane didn't crash, and then that's it. Left alone, he will imagine you in all kinds of exotic circumstances, and nothing you actually tell him will in any way compare to the amazing stuff his fantasy version of you is doing.

If You Feel He's Slip-Sliding Away

If you feel yourself getting neurotic after you've had sex with him, you must act immediately. Don't allow your insecurity to snowball. Follow my twelve-step plan.

1. Establish scientifically if you really are losing your grip on him, or just on reality

Start keeping a diary. Just write a few notes after every date with him. Then, one evening when you're feeling rational and sane, get it out and look through all the entries. Look for stuff like the frequency of his phone calls, presents he's bought, whether he's started cancelling dates, whether he still emails you every day . . . Don't focus on one thing in particular, but get a proper feel of how things are progressing, or stalling. Keep in mind anything stressful he might have had going on in his life, like work pressures, or money worries or whatever. Girls are hopeless at remembering that men sometimes have to deal with life stuff.

Now, looking at this rationally: does it seem like his attentiveness to you is on a sharp decline? Yes? Then follow the next steps – they'll perk him up. No? Follow the next steps anyway, as they'll make sure he doesn't get bored. Not sure? Then take time to think about how *you* tend to be in relationships. Do you often hit a wobbly, unconfident stage after the initial beginning? Have most of your boyfriends at one point said things to you like, 'Of *course* I love you, now let go of my ankle'? Do your friends tend not to pay attention to your relationship dramas anymore, but just tell you that you worry too much? Do you tend to lack confidence in everything, not just your love life? Are you, in fact, a bit bonkers? Do the following steps and, if you *still* feel shaky, buy a good book on NLP, like *Feeling Good* by Dr David Burns. NLP is a therapy that trains your brain to stop thinking the same old negative things about yourself and your life. It stands for Neuro Linguistic Programming, but could equally stand for 'Nuke Love Psychosis' because that's what it also does.

2. Boost your own confidence

Most of us tend to get our confidence from the men we're dating, which is terrible because when they chuck us for being a high-maintenance nutcase we're immediately back to square one. So you need to get your own self-confidence in place first.

Easy ways to boost your confidence:

- **Exercise.** Twenty minutes a day is enough to make your brain start producing feel-good endorphins, but thirty minutes a day will make you look better naked, so decide now whether your self-loathing comes from low brain chemicals or mirrors. When you feel low, throw on your trainers and go for a long walk.
- **Review your successes.** Make a list of everything you feel proud of about yourself. This could be career-based ('I

was the first woman in my department to be promoted to manager'), social-based ('Twenty-five people came to my birthday party last year'), beauty-based ('Almost nothing came out on my last pore strip') – whatever you like. Don't feel you have to list only those things that other people would admire in you. For example, if you're less impressed with your career triumphs than the fact you taught yourself to raise one eyebrow, list the eyebrow instead.

- **Do a compliment swap-shop.** Find an equally unconfident friend and tease her till she cries! No, sorry – find an equally unconfident friend and spend an evening listing things you love about each other. Write them all down so you can gloat over your list later. Don't be tempted to do this with your man – at the first hint of him starting to run low on nice things about you, you'll feel suicidal.

3. Change the chemicals in your head

You can do this with exercise, see above, but you can also do it through dancing until you feel ecstatic, watching a DVD that really makes you laugh, or doing something lovely for someone else. Volunteer work is one of the best ways to uplift your mood.

4. Don't see him for a week

If your levels of insecurity are getting out of hand, or if you just want to cool things down for a bit and regroup, you can take a mini break from the relationship and not see him for a while. I know this feels terrifying if you're besotted, and you're scared that he'll either chuck you or meet someone else, but let's be rational about this. If you were seeing a man you weren't that bothered about, you'd probably happily not see him for a bit if you were really busy, wouldn't you? In fact, you probably wouldn't think twice about not seeing him for a month, or a lifetime. And rationally, you know that that wouldn't put him off. In fact, it would only make him keener.

Well, that's exactly what'll happen with a man you *are* bothered about. I repeat: it's only different because you like him. If you're really starting to go slightly nuts over a man, that is the perfect time to pull back. The next time you meet up, you'll find that his increased attentiveness is just the antidote to your anxiety. But if it's not, you can always . . .

5. Be the Incredible Vanishing Woman

This is only to be used if a man is really slacking off and making you worry. It's the emergency Axe of Love that you only bring out for a good reason.

Good reasons to disappear are: he stands you up, he only rings you for Booty Calls, he forgets or ignores major events like your birthday or Valentine's Day, he breaks a promise to you (over something big, like picking you up from the airport, not something minor like never calling you during *Pop Idol*), he flirts outrageously with another woman in front of you, or he abandons you at a party. Inexcusable behaviour, in short. When this happens, just end the date (if you're on one at the time) as quickly as possible and then don't answer his calls or emails or texts for a fortnight. Don't complain, don't explain, just vanish.

During this period of no contact, he'll be forced to think about what he did, and he will realize that you aren't going to stand for being treated this way. He'll see, with perfect clarity and living proof, that you're not going to put up with crap and he'll fix the problem all on his own. The next time you surface and talk to him, he'll be desperate to see you and make it up to you. And he'll do it all by himself.

6. Learn something new

When your man isn't doing anything wrong, but you just want to stop *thinking* about him *every second of the day*, sign up for classes in something. It's the best way to stop the constant circulation of thoughts about a man, because you have to concentrate and take in information. This is far more effective than just seeing your friends for drinks or whatever, because we all know that if you see your friends you'll just end up talking about your boyfriend.

When I was single, I used to take tennis lessons when I found myself having obsessive thoughts about men. I should be Wimbledon-ready by now, it happened that often. For that one hour a week, I finally thought about something else. It's not the getting outside that does it, or the meeting new people, although they both help too – it's the having to concentrate on learning stuff. Obviously don't take anything too sex-related, like massage classes, or you'll only want to try out your new moves on your boyfriend as soon as you get out. Instead, try something slightly complicated and technical, like sewing lessons, pilates, or advanced yoga.

7. Stop being exclusive

If you took my advice about multiple-dating, you could start it again if your boyfriend's behaviour doesn't exactly match the dictionary definition of 'cherishing'. You don't need a big long *talk* about it. Just one evening, mention that you're not happy with your 'exclusive' status, and think you should lighten things up a bit and go back to just 'dating' each other, and other people.

Only do this if you're unhappy, not as a punishment. Punishments don't work. Only do this if you're getting upset by the way he's treating you and want to put some space back into the relationship for the sake of your sanity.

8. Stop the sex

Look at me, just casually tossing this tip in with all the others like it's no big deal. 'Oh, just stop shagging him,' she types airily, waving a hand around. 'He won't mind a bit, and it's bound to help him see sense.'

I have to admit, stopping sex mid-stream is never as good as simply never having it in the first place. But if you really feel taken for granted, it can help centre you, and sometimes it's effective in making a man realize what he might be losing. When a girlfriend stops making love, her boyfriend will be forced to imagine that the relationship itself might be ending next.

If you're going to try this, do it calmly and confidently. Go through your reasons beforehand so you feel sure of why you're doing it. But don't lay all those reasons on him, as he'll just desperately search for logical-sounding replies to each one and you'll start questioning yourself. Just say something vague like, 'I'm not comfortable at the moment, and until I am, I'd rather not have sex.' Or you can just stop any sleepover dates for a couple of weeks, saying, 'I'm tired, I'm afraid I [or 'you'] can't stay tonight, but I'll see you next week.' As soon as you're not Little Miss Sure-Thing, your man will either realize he hasn't got you 100 per cent and step up his pursuit, or he'll wander off to the next guaranteed shag. Whichever way, you will feel better. Trust me, you'll feel better. Yes you will. Yes, yes, yes you will.

9. Make a big goal for the coming year

This is a great way to drag your wandering, bloke-obsessed thoughts back to the main focus of your life, which is *you*. Think back to your childhood self. What were your big dreams? Did you want to be an air stewardess, help orphans in Borneo, write books, be an illustrator? Choose one and take steps towards it.

What usually happens is that you are just getting all revved-up at home, plotting how you're going to be the first woman to swim topless across the Atlantic, when your man calls you. They can *smell* when you're thinking about something else.

And be positive and enthusiastic about your goals when you're with your bloke. Don't play them down, or refuse to talk about them in case he feels *threatened*. He won't – he'll see the light behind your eyes and get really keen on you all over again. Which is obviously not the reason to *have* goals, but it's a nice side-effect.

10. Change five things in your life

These can be tiny, but try five of the following:

- changing your route to work;
- rearranging your furniture (there's an old saying: *Change the direction of your bed, change the direction of your life*. Try it and see if it works.);
- buying a weird new brand of coffee;
- putting a pot-plant on your desk in the office;
- trying out a new author;
- only watching BBC2 all night;
- buying a goldfish;
- only drinking red drinks in the pub;

- learning poker;
- reading a different newspaper every day;
- only eating yellow food for a day;
- looking up old friends online and emailing them.

You get the idea. These are small changes. All you're doing is focussing on you again. Nothing massive and life-changing like emigrating to New Zealand, but little things that just lift your spirits and stop you ringing your man to discuss the relationship.

11. Beautify yourself

You physically cannot feel worried about a relationship after you have had a haircut, manicure and pedicure, applied fake tan and gone to bed at 9pm. It's medically *impossible* to analyse if he is slipping away from you as you do a shoe-trade with an equal-sized friend. You can't mope and steam your pores simultaneously. You can't cry while you have a bikini wax (well, in fact you can't *not* cry while having a bikini wax, but at least you're not crying over him).

12. Chuck him

Sometimes, a girl's just got to dump the chump. And really, if after making positive changes in your life, pulling back, focussing on yourself and ripping your moustache out with a bulldog clip, your man is STILL the cause of your insecurity and anxiety, just finish it.

Again, so easy for me to say. But it's also easy to do, if you believe the Universal Truths of Dating:

1. There is always another man.
2. Each boyfriend you have is usually better than the one before.

If you don't believe me, ponder the list of boyfriends that you've had throughout your whole life. From the first one to your current one, write them down. (Listen to me and my constant requests for you to write stuff down. Anyone would think I'm just trying to keep your hands busy so you can't go calling any boys.) Haven't they all been better than the one before? They have. You need to look at them objectively and coldly, but you'll see that you usually date *upwards*.

So why hang on to a man who doesn't make you feel brilliant when you're with him? There is zero reason. Especially as hanging around with Misery Guts is only stopping you from flinging on a new dress, applying frosted shadow underneath your eyebrows and waltzing off with your two best girlfriends to the very next Speed Dating event you can find.

Question Time

This sounds like hard work. Can't I just be myself now we're having sex? I think if he gets to be inside my body, he should know what's going on inside my head, too.

You are so very, very young.

I'm not telling you to ditch him or stop having sex if things are going wonderfully and you've never been happier – only if things are making you worried and anxious.

What I'm trying to do is help you focus on yourself, and realize that a boyfriend should only be a small part of your otherwise busy and fulfilled life. When you pull back and start taking an interest in your life again, your man sits up and discovers for himself that if he treats you lazily, you'll leave because you have lots of other options.

Am I ever allowed to be myself and tell him what I'm thinking, or what I'm worried about?

Yes, of course you're allowed to be the real you. None of this is about hiding your personality or being someone else. It's about protecting yourself so you don't waste years on relationships that aren't going anywhere.

Also, don't necessarily feel that the 'real' you has to be someone who expresses every thought that crosses her mind. If telling a man that he shouldn't eye up other women in your company (for example) would actually do any good, I'd be all for it. But if a man is selfish and clueless enough to do that, it's better for you that he *keeps* doing it, because you'll get to find out sooner that he is selfish and clueless and probably not the best man for you. Why would you want to date someone whom you have to mend?

If I stop having sex with him, he is soooo going to chuck me.

Good. If he does, he's only staying with you to get a regular, easy porking and has no respect for your feelings. Better that he does chuck you and you're forced to date other people until you find someone who feels lucky just to hold your hand. You know, you *will* find someone like that – the trick is not to stop looking before he comes along.

7

☆ut of the Mouths of Men

My friends would copulate with anything that moved, but I never saw any reason to limit myself.

Emo Phillips

It takes two to do the horizontal hokey-cokey, so we can't have a book on abstinence without getting the male point of view. After all, the object of withholding sex until commitment is to *get* the commitment. We're not going through all this self-work only to end up exactly where we started but with cleaner sheets.

When I started this book, I knew from personal experience that men liked girls who said 'No'. But after talking to many men, from cads to dads, I was still surprised at the overwhelming tide of approval.

It's *women* who don't like saying 'No'. Partly due to fear that they will never meet a man who sticks around without getting something in return; partly due to low self-esteem –

thinking they're not enough to interest anyone when they're dressed; partly due to resentment at the double-standard; partly due to the false intimacy nookie can bring; and partly due to the fact that sex is really, really nice.

Men have remained unchanged through the winds of feminism. If they noticed anything at all, it's that women seem a bit grumpier, didn't wear bras for a bit (cool!) and now aren't as much of a challenge. Of course, they'll never admit this to anyone with whom they secretly hope to have a bunk-up, so I've collected their thoughts here on your behalf.

Who Men Will Have Sex With

Men are depressingly open about being literally up to bonk anything. I assumed that men had standards. Lower than ours, of course, but still firmly in place. Instead:

> Would I shag anyone? Yes. Most men would. When we're having a poker evening and are sitting around talking man-to-man or something, all of us agree that, pretty much, 'every hole's a goal' but it's not something we advertise to the ladies. I have a close female friend that I can talk to about anyone and we were discussing this the other day. We were at a kids' play centre and it was full of women. She was pointing at them, one by one, saying 'Her?' and my answer was always 'yes'. Even if the

women were twenty years older than me, or obviously not my type, I would always have sex with them.

James, 32, long-term relationship

Men have sex indiscriminately, but only when it won't mean anything. We tend to categorize women into 'short-term' and 'long-term'. You could look at a girl and know immediately she doesn't have what you're looking for long-term, but you would still have sex with her, because it satisfies your short-term itch. When you're at a nightclub, often you'll deliberately target the less attractive women or the ones wearing tarty clothes, because you think you'd have more chance of scoring with them that night than you would with a prettier girl. You think that the prettier girls will think more of themselves than to go home with a bloke from a nightclub.

Simon, 41, married

If you're looking for a long-term girlfriend, you would probably be less likely to have sex with girls you don't fancy in the meantime. Actually no, forget that. That's a lie.

Jonathan, 23, in a relationship

Would most men shag anyone? Darling, most men would shag a watermelon with a hole in it.

Mark, 38, long-term relationship

Would I have sex with a girl I didn't find attractive? Yes. Why? Because they all feel the same inside. It's nicer if you like looking at their face but if you don't, it still *feels* good. You're just more likely to do it doggy-style.

Oliver, 46, single

This is backed up with scientific research, so we can't console ourselves with the fact that some men – a tiny handful, probably with just a tiny handful down their trousers – are the only ones out there bonking women they don't like. American studies of male mating 'strategies' have revealed that men will lower their standards substantially to increase the range of potential short-term mates. Men also use strategies to decide which woman is most likely to have sex with them after the shortest investment of time. If a woman is dressed provocatively, uses sexual language or approaches men, instead of waiting to be approached, she is judged to be an easy target. In fact, 'there is some evidence that men pursuing short-term mating ... prefer women who have sexual experience and avoid women who appear prudish or low in sex drive,' say Haselton and Buss. Which *finally* explains why I've never pulled in a polo-neck.

When to Have Sex

Men agreed that the first date was too soon to have sex – *unless that's all they wanted from the girl in the first place*. If that was the case, they liked having first-date nookie because it saved them from having to shell out for more dinners.

> When I've been on first dates with a girl who has made it very clear, usually by provocative comments, that sex is on the cards, I feel a sinking feeling in my stomach. It's like, 'Here we go again.' Don't get me wrong, I love sex, but just once it would be nice to meet a girl who lets the excitement build slowly. The early part of dating should be the time to let the sexual tension build up gradually. Like, when you're crossing the street and your hand brushes against hers, that can be exciting in itself when it's the first time. But it dulls the excitement if just twenty minutes ago you'd been using that hand to play with her.
>
> Nick, 36, single

> If I like the girl, I feel relieved and pleased if she ends the date with a brief kiss on the cheek. It's nice to meet a woman who values herself.
>
> Dan, 28, living with girlfriend

I met a woman at work who made it clear in the office that she fancied me. I was trying to explain something to her and she kept staring at my mouth until I finally said, 'Listen, let's go out for a drink tonight. Now will you please concentrate on what I'm saying?' We went out and I was having a great time, until she suddenly said, 'I have to do something,' and leaned over and snogged me. At that moment I knew sex would be on the cards. Because I liked her, I tried to explain that I sometimes preferred not to have sex on the first date. She said she agreed, then invited me back to her house, saying I was welcome to sleep on the sofa. When we got back to her tiny flat, the sofa had a huge Doberman on it, giving me a look that said: 'I don't know where you think you're sleeping.' So the girl said I could share her bed but nothing would happen. I made a great play of pushing down the duvet between us to create a 'safe space', then she came out of the bathroom wearing a T-shirt with nothing underneath. I explained again that I liked to wait for sex if I liked the girl, because it ruined it if we just shagged immediately. She agreed, then climbed on top of me. What's a man supposed to do? We had sex, but in the morning I jokingly – but honestly – told her she'd blown her chances with me.

Neil, 30, married

Of course you don't always want to wait. Sometimes you're not in the market for a long-term thing, in which case first-night sex is *exactly* what you're looking for.

Daniel, 36, married

I've found that the women who have sex on the first few dates generally turn out to have self-esteem issues. I don't judge women's self-confidence by when they sleep with me. But looking back, the needier girls put out the earliest.

Mack, 50, married

That last quote reminds me of an episode of Channel Four's *Peepshow* where the male lead is talking to a woman he's fancied for years. During the conversation she makes a few self-derogatory remarks and he thinks, 'Beautiful *and* low self-esteem – I've hit the motherload!'

How Long a Wait is too Long?

Men are agreed on one thing: waiting is boring when you don't like the girl. It's also boring when you do like the girl, but not boring enough to make them stop.

If I wasn't that into the girl, I'd see her a few times without shagging her. But not that long. Two weeks? Three?

Something like that. If she still wasn't having any of it, I'd move on to someone else.

Oliver, 34, dating

When a girl won't sleep with me on the first date, I'm not that surprised. If she still hasn't by the third date, I start to think of her as a challenge. But then, if I'm not really getting to like her after about a month, I'll drop her.

Sam, 24, single

If you're not that bothered about a girl, you're going to wait a month, maximum. But if you were really keen and you knew she wanted to wait, you'd do it as long as she needed. However, you would need a definite reason why she wanted to wait. After a while the question becomes, 'Why hasn't sex happened yet?' It's the elephant in the corner nobody talks about. If her answer is always vague, you'd start to think she probably didn't like you. But if you knew she had religious or moral reasons, you could quite happily carry on. I suppose you just don't want to be used while she gets over someone else.

Paul, 36, married

See how they weed themselves out quickly? These same men admitted they would date a girl for a sexual relationship 'indefinitely; until I went off her or met someone better' which could take months. And all that time, the girl is practising her married signature and not meeting anyone else.

But there's a difference between a man pressuring you and just being really, really enthusiastic about the idea of sex:

> With my first girlfriend, we both agreed to wait until the time was right. At first we were in synch with all of this, but after about three months I decided that, you know, maybe I was ready. However, she preferred to wait a bit longer. So then, every time we went on a date I'd ask her, 'Is the time right yet?' This went on for another four months, every time her replying, 'Not quite yet. Soon.' Eventually, after a wedding, we were sitting in the pub, both all dressed up in our best clothes. Just half-jokingly I asked her, 'Is the time right yet?' fully expecting the same reply. But she said, 'Yes, I think it is.' I was like, 'Come on, then! Sup up!'
>
> Stuart, 35, dating

Still, there was a common consensus that when a man loves a woman, he'll not only sleep out in the rain, he'll wait as long as she needs to feel comfortable.

> When you love someone, you want them to be happy, don't you? You're not going to force them to do something they don't want to do.
>
> Mark, 38, long-term relationship

If I knew the woman had real reasons for wanting to wait, like she was old-fashioned or religious, I'd wait a lot longer than if I felt she was testing me in some way. If I was in love with her, it wouldn't bother me to wait if waiting made her happy.

Keith, 45, married

I waited two years before my wife and I had sex. When we met she was dating someone else so I had to make a real play to 'win' her. Then she said she preferred not to rush into anything. That was fine with me. I wanted to prove to her that I was interested in her, not just sex. I'd already had plenty of that! I'm not saying it wasn't hard to do, but that's just how our relationship happened. It took me six months to get a proper kiss. But it was worth the wait. That was a really good kiss.

John, 45, married

I knew my wife wanted to wait until she got married to have sex, but as it turned out we ended up not doing it until three months after the wedding. She broke her leg on honeymoon when she got hit by a motorbike.

Stephen, 33, married

It's like buying a house. You know the minute you walk in whether or not you're going to buy it. Same with women. I think you both know if the 'click' is there at the start. And if it's not, you're not going to hang around. But if it is, nothing the girl can do will put you off. If it's just a question of waiting a few months – no problem.

Dan, 48, married

Men Follow the Woman's Lead

A man might try it on with you, but he still knows that it is *your decision* when the security gates come off your underwear. Don't let yourself feel guilted into having early sex. No man expects to get lucky. It's just a hope. An incredibly strong, yearning hope. A hope that burns stronger than the Sun. The hope that gets him out of bed and into the shower every morning. But still just a hope.

Women can't have sex as easily as men, there are repercussions, like pregnancy. We know this. But if a woman shows herself to be 'up for it', we're not going to turn her down. That might sound hypocritical, but a woman has to figure out for herself if she's willing to risk her future for a quickie.

Paul, 33, single

I definitely took my lead from girls when I was single – I always waited for them to show they were ready to have sex. Which is funny, because when I got married, the roles completely reversed.

Ben, 35, married

However, men sometimes try to encourage the woman to wait a while. Like Nick, on page 142, men are realizing that waiting before they have sex can make the whole relationship more special. Sadly, it often has the opposite effect. Women seem to find men who say 'No' incredibly hot, by and large.

You're going to think I'm gay, but I have actually told a girl I really liked that we didn't have to sleep together yet. That we could wait a while to make it even more special. It's weird to realize that I am actually pushier for sex with girls I don't like! I suppose I wanted to show the girl that I could be more evolved than the type of bloke who just wants a f**k. This has only happened once, however. We ended up doing it that night anyway, but then we lived together for several years.

Graham, 42, living with a girlfriend

We'd had a sleepover and my girlfriend was the friskier one that evening. I said, 'No, let's do it when the time is perfect.' This was a lot to do with the fact that I'd been drinking and didn't know if I'd be much good, if I'm honest. But we'd already waited for six or seven weeks and it seemed silly to blow it all by having a half-drunk shag on a Tuesday night. She was insistent but I resisted. However, when she tried again the next morning, it was Game Over. I did my best, I'm only human. What was I meant to do? Stick it in the freezer?

Steve, 31, living with girlfriend

Men Do Try to be Good

Most men – the decent types, not die-hard players – often try to do the right thing. It's just that, well, they're not always the ones doing the thinking.

I feel that I have more responsibility towards women I've had sex with. So I try not to shag someone I'm not interested in. I try not to ... but sometimes, when I've been drinking, or it's the heat of the moment, or I'm feeling particularly, er, 'het up', I have to admit that the voices in my head reminding me of my moral stance do get fainter. Um, not that I have voices in my head, you understand.

Andy, 37, single

I have never led on a woman. She just doesn't read the signs. Here is the news, girls: if a man isn't taking you outside in the fresh air occasionally, doesn't buy you presents, only calls after 9pm and finds excuses not to take you to big parties – he doesn't like you. If I do all that, is it my fault if the woman doesn't read the writing on the wall?

Tom, 33, single

Most Men Don't See a Big Difference Between Heavy Petting and Sex

This was the biggest shock to me. When I started this book, I thought that there was a huge difference between oral sex and sex. I even had a theory about it – that it was biological evolution, and that men can't ever feel they have 'conquered' a woman until they might possibly have inseminated her. I was so wrong.

When I say I prefer a woman who takes it slowly, I mean someone who doesn't kiss me full-on, with tongues, for the first few months. Oral sex counts as sex, of course it does. Even using your hands counts – it's just sex using another part of your body.

Nick, 36, single

If a woman had told me she prefers to wait for sex then dropped to her knees and gave me a blowjob, I'd feel she was selling out on her principles. What's the difference?

Toby, 29, living with girlfriend

Not all men felt this way, but it was more than half. Some felt the chase was still on until they had scored a home run, like this charmer:

> When you've had oral from a girl, you know that full sex is in the post. From that moment it's just a matter of days. What I especially like to do is give the girl oral sex. I haven't met one yet that has the strength of will to turn down sex after I've made her come with my mouth.
>
> Andy, 32, single

Men will never admit to any woman that this is how they really think. Even if they don't want to have sex with you personally, many of them seem to keep a Code of Silence in case you hear anything that might put you off having sex with another bachelor. If you ever need hard-core sensible dating advice, always ask a man who doesn't want to shag you. Dads are the obvious choices of course, as are brothers, distant uncles or gay best friends. Never ask a bachelor. He'll only tell you what your boyfriend wants you to hear.

When I worked at a men's magazine I got a great insight into the male mind and how low it can go. Of course, all men aren't bastards; often they worry unnecessarily about hurting women's feelings. For example, they're usually wracked with guilt about having to finish with a girlfriend, even if she is actually going to sob with happiness and relief when they do. I think this is where the trouble starts – to avoid causing us pain, they lie by omission. Few men will look you in the eye and say, 'I love you' if they don't. But even fewer will ever greet you for the first time with, 'Hi, I'm John and you're totally not my type, but I feel a bit randy. How about we hook up for nookie for about three weeks, then I'll disappear from your life completely? What do you say?'

If in doubt, don't. So, if you ever want to know how a man truly sees you, do nothing. Don't call him, don't ask him out and – if I need to repeat this – don't take anything off. Let men's laziness work in your favour.

8

I Told You So (Success Stories)

> *Pre-1989 I pretty much f**ked everybody. I had to get breakfast somehow.*
>
> Courtney Love

Just as men love nothing more than to shag and brag, women who have kept their knickers on love to not shag and brag. So here, to strengthen your resolve, are the success stories I've collected from the women I interviewed for this book.

Warning

Reading happy-ever-after stories when you have just crawled out of your bedroom after an eighteen-hour shagathon with an uncommitted boyfriend can seriously kill your buzz. We do not recommend reading this material if you are of a regretful nature, due to injuries caused by kicking yourself. Due to the unashamed smugness of these women, I have awarded these stories a PG (Pure Gloating) Rating.

My best tips are: decide before your date how far you're prepared to go, and then stick to it. No letting him convince you otherwise! And write down your reasons for waiting, and read them often. I read mine after every date with the man who's now my husband.

Katie, 36

Why is abstinence – something that brings such peace and dignity to a woman – such a taboo subject? It should be celebrated!

Danielle, 40

I was what you would call late to the party when it came to waiting to have sex. I grew up in the Feminist era, and we all thought at college that having casual sex was the ultimate in freedom. None of us minded if we never got married, because there seemed to be very few men whom we'd want to tie ourselves to permanently.

So, most of my twenties were spent drifting from man to man. I was so focussed on getting what I thought I wanted from relationships that I didn't bother to notice what the men were giving me. In fact, because I was so vehemently anti-marriage, three men proposed to me after we'd had sex, which I took to be proof that all those ideas about 'some you bed and some you wed' were out-dated.

When I hit thirty my feelings started to change, because I realized I wanted children and I didn't want to bring kids into the world without being married to their dad. So I started dating more seriously, openly talking about marriage and kids. You have never seen men run away so fast! I took this as further proof of the patriarchy.

When I was thirty-four I met a man at a feminist rally. He seemed sensitive and intuitive, my perfect match. We had sex on the third date, and things progressed smoothly. Soon we were seeing each other every night. After a year I asked him where he saw things going, and he asked me to move in with him, which I did. As I was thirty-five then, I thought living together would move us towards marriage but it seemed to go the opposite way. He started staying out later and I'd often sit in the kitchen and cry, looking at the dinner I'd cooked him. I'd become the woman I despised in my twenties. After a few more go-nowhere months I asked him point-blank about marriage. He ummed and aahed but wouldn't commit to a date. I left that night.

As I licked my wounds on a girlfriend's sofa, I vowed that I was off men for good. I'd started looking into insemination clinics when a man from work asked me out. I kept putting him off because he wasn't my 'type' – too macho. He persisted and we eventually went out for a drink. He brought me flowers, which I accidentally left in the pub! He went back and got them. He pursued me hard for four or five months but I was still pretty ambiguous about him, so I didn't have sex. I wasn't consciously waiting – I just didn't want to get into another relationship. About six months in, he brought up the subject and I told him, jokingly, I was saving myself for marriage. Three weeks later he turned up at my house with a ring and a proposal.

Since then, I've noticed how my more old-fashioned girlfriends get married more quickly than my feminist friends. I still believe in feminism but I also can't believe how much easier relationships go without sex. I'm now pregnant at last with our first child.

Sharon, 39

If a man tells you how hard the waiting is for him, tell him that he shouldn't be talking to you about it. His frustration is something to talk to the guys about.

Anita, 36

When I made the decision to wait, I was saying to myself – I'm not ashamed of my femininity anymore. I'm not trying to hide that part of me that gets hurt. My softness as a woman isn't to be ashamed of – it's something to cherish, something to protect.

Georgina, 32

I was telling my married sister the other day how my boyfriend had just taken me to look at rings! She stared at me, and said: 'Have you had sex with the poor man yet?' and I laughingly said, 'No!' She couldn't believe it. She just kept shaking her head in disbelief. Finally her husband chimed in: 'It's *because* they haven't had sex that he is so keen to snap her up.'

Juliet, 22

Men aren't frightened of commitment. This is something that women have made up to explain away the guys that don't love them. Men do want commitment, but only with a woman who challenges them.

Fran, 32

After my husband proposed to me, he mentioned my decision to wait before having sex. He said it made him appreciate my 'uniqueness', that it made me 'different to other girls – better'. I often caught him looking at me in this contemplative way when we were dating, especially if other girls around us were acting more forwardly than I ever did.

Mary, 37

Abstinence isn't a guarantee against break-ups. But it is a guarantee against giving something of yourself to a man who later rejects it.

Caroline, 45

As my brother told me, men don't want an easy girl. They'll take her, if she's offering herself, but they really want a woman who values herself enough not to offer herself to any man.

Martine, 25

I had sex with my first husband on the third date, which at the time felt like forever! We still got married but, looking back, he was never that cherishing towards me. We were more like really close friends. Eventually that fizzled out – we were very young when we married – and I started dating again. A friend had been reading *A Return to Modesty* [a US book that advocates waiting until marriage before having sex] and she asked me if I'd support her in her decision – i.e. be there for her to call if she was ever in her house with a man and too tempted! I decided I'd go one further and abstain too. To be honest, I was lukewarm about marrying again so felt it would be no great loss if I put anyone off. I dated four men who were all very interested until I told them I was waiting, then they disappeared. Then I started dating Tom. I remember telling him very jadedly quite early on that I wasn't into uncommitted sex anymore. I expected him to up and leave the restaurant! But he just looked me in the eyes and said, 'I'll wait.' That was so sexy and manly I almost had sex then! But we carried on dating and he treated me so differently to my first husband. He's much more willing to listen to my feelings, and he always acts in a very protective way. About six weeks into dating Tom, one of the 'amazing disappearing men' (as my girlfriend and I called them) reappeared on the scene saying he was wrong to stop calling me. I agreed with him, then ended the call. Tom proposed after three months. I thought that was too soon, so made him wait another three months. By that point I knew I could never get anyone who loved me more, so I accepted. We've been married six years now and he makes me happy every single day.

Susan, 43

The world is full of men who will date women who don't sleep with them. They're everywhere. You just might be the first person who's ever made them wait.

Samantha, 35

Panic Stations! Last Tips to Avoid Temptation

A word about oral contraception. I asked a girl to go to bed with me, she said 'no'.

Woody Allen

Emergency! Emergency! We've got a live one! This is the chapter to bear in mind before you bare your behind. Sometimes, on a first date – or even a twenty-first date – the urge to romp comes over you like a steamroller and you've just got to have that man *now*. Even when you've read all the advice in this book, there's still a part of you (and I think you know which part I mean) that screams, 'Oh sod it – just do him! Do him hard!'

That's natural, because we are not programmed to withhold ourselves when there's a man in our bedroom, it's way past midnight and every hormone in our bodies is telling us to jump on top of him and perform the Reverse Cowgirl with Rodeo Grip.

But please try to remember this chapter. Take it into the bathroom and read it whilst you splash water on your face and run your wrists under the cold tap. Keep it by the bedside table and reach for it with one trembling hand while you do God-knows-what with the other. Or memorize it and replay it whenever there's something sitting on the bed that isn't a stuffed teddy-bear. After that, you're on your own. I've done all I can.

First Date Nerves

I've got a first date tonight and there's no way I'll be able to keep my mitts off him. He's 100 per cent my type and just gorgeous.

This is exactly the time to keep your mitts off him! Play your cards right by exercising some self-discipline and letting him see you as maddeningly elusive, and you could end up leaping into bed next to him every night for the rest of your life.

Tips:

- Wear your worst underwear. You know the ones I mean. The pair you would rather chew off and eat rather than let any man see.
- Eat a heavy dinner. Loads of starch – potatoes, pasta,

bread. This will make your stomach blow up like a hot-air balloon and therefore put you off getting naked.

Second Date Nerves

Our first date was okay, but not amazing. I was wondering – if I actually don't like him that much, is it all right to sleep with him? It's not like I'll be risking alienating my future husband.

I can understand this line of thought. When you don't think you like a man that much, it seems a lot less risky to wander off the Path of Virtue towards the Woods of Temptation, because what have you got to lose? He's just an okay bloke and if he goes off you, so what? You were never that bothered anyway.

Except, women fall in love more slowly than men do. If at the end of the first date you weren't immediately stricken with the urge to write, 'Dear Diary, Tonight I met my future husband,' it doesn't mean that you won't actually fall madly in love with him in another few weeks. You know what we're like, we're fickle. One night we can't stand someone, but the next we're suddenly writhing with jealousy when we catch him sneaking shifty glances towards our flatmate.

Besides, those 'slow-burning' men are often the ones we should end up with. The nice men, who don't set our knickers on fire on the first date, are almost always the best men for us. They're nicer, sweeter, and don't cause us to go off the rails with blind adoration. They're good bets.

So, don't think I'm going to let you tear off your top just because you don't think he's Mr Right. It's STILL a good idea to wait – firstly because you might end up really liking him, and secondly because you want to get out of the habit of having casual sex. We're trying to break your pattern here, remember? And practice makes perfect. It'll be easier to keep your knickers on with all the men you meet in future if you haven't weakened their elastic by tearing them off with men you kid yourself 'don't count'.

Tips:

- Don't talk yourself into sex. Even if it's been a few months since you had a bonk, don't let your lust-crazed brain invent reasons for getting horizontal.
- Only accept dates that you know will be chaste. Public places are safe, unless you're an exhibitionist.
- Don't drink too much. For one thing, you'll remain in control. For another, he'll remain only mildly attractive.
- Aim to be back at your place – alone – before midnight. If this is hard for you, only make dates on school-nights and use the weekends for getting out to meet more men for your Rotation.

Third Date Nerves

This is the point where I usually crack. Remind me why I'm trying to stay chaste again?

Because you want to be adored. Three dates feels like a long time when you're with a man you like (or a really long time with a man you hate), but it's not long enough to assess his character. You want a man who *adores* you. Unless he has already proposed, keep your knickers on.

Tips:

- Turn down any requests he makes to either come back to your place or take you back to his. This will not look weird. He is not your estate agent.
- End the date first. Three hours is perfectly long enough. Think, 'Less is More, More is Whore'.
- Concentrate on one thing you despise about him. Can't find anything? Think about him on the toilet. Not bad enough? Think about him being sick. Still not enough? Think about him going home and telling his friends tomorrow morning, 'Yes! See, I told you I could have her. Where's my £20?' Re-read Chapter Seven. Men *are* that bad.

Fourth Date Nerves

I could tell that my date was slightly surprised when we didn't have sex on the Third Date, so now I'm worried he will *definitely* expect some tonight. What should I do?

Nothing. His expectations are nothing for you to worry yourself over. You're not some anatomically correct sex product he ordered online, which comes with a guarantee – you're a living, breathing, saying 'No' girl. It's up to you when to do it.

This smacks to me of Brittle Backbone Disease. I know it's very easy to fret over a man's happiness, trying to climb inside his brain and see what's happening in there, but it's a habit I'd urge you to break. As soon as we start worrying what a man is thinking we start to tinker subtly with our own behaviour, tweaking it to correspond to what he might want. That quickly becomes addictive, until you end up not knowing where you end and he begins. Ugh. You can't control his expectations, so just carry on doing what you want to do. If you'd be happier ending tonight on a chaste note (and, really, you would be), go ahead and do that. If he was intrigued by a sex-free Third Date, he'll be practically obsessed by a sex-free Fourth Date. He'll really start to see you as someone different.

Tips:

- Be on your guard for any of his 'big guns' coming out. These could be suggestions like 'Hey, wanna try one of my famous massages?' or 'You look tired, why don't you sleep at my place tonight?' He won't actually come right out with 'Oh, PLEASE let me shag you' but that's what he means. Smilingly refuse any offer that involves you taking anything off.

- Don't bring anything along to the date that might help you get ready in the morning. So no extra make-up, no spare tights, no toothbrush. Sometimes we 'accidentally' slip stuff like this into our handbag kidding ourselves it's just in case our car breaks down. The only thing you *are* allowed to bring is taxi money, so you can always get home.

Fifth Date Nerves

I'm being very virginal, but the sexual chemistry with my boyfriend is insane! Even before I meet him I can feel myself getting over-excited. I really like him, and my hormones are going berserk. I can't hold out much longer.

Whoa, Nelly. Okay, you two are letting the physical attraction over-whelm everything else. You need to take a breather and do dates that are more intellectual.

Tips:

- Do brainier activities, like go to a pub quiz together, go to the theatre, or go to a coffee shop and play backgammon. Keep your mind busier and it won't have time to gurgle thoughts such as 'I wonder what your inner thigh tastes like?'
- Only accept a date when it has a definite activity planned. (NOT that one.) I mean, don't just agree the day and time and then meet up and 'see what happens'. Try to make sure there are tickets booked, if possible. Left alone and plan-less, you two will be happily humping in seconds.

Sixth Date Nerves

Everything is going well, and I like the way he's treating me. Only, sex does seem to come up a lot in conversation. It's just little mentions now and again. Things like he heard his neighbours having wild nookie last night, or he just read in *Maxim* that every orgasm lengthens your lifespan by five minutes. I don't know how to reply.

Don't take it too seriously. All this means is that sex is on his mind. And of course it is – it always is. Men are meant to think about sex an average of six times an hour, which I think is a conservative estimate. Now he's not having sex, it's on his mind even more. The inside of his mind looks like an episode of *Hollyoaks: After Hours*.

He might be bringing up the subject as casually as he can to find out your views on it. (This happens a lot before The Talk.) He mentions his neighbours' night of passion to see how you reply, whether it's 'Oh that poor girl, she is being heartlessly used by that cad' or 'Really? Phwoargh! I could do with a good shagging myself!' Or he quotes the *Maxim* statistic to open a Heated Debate on Sex and Its Proven Health Benefits. He's not trying to hassle you, he just wants to know what you're planning for him.

Tips:

- If possible, try to treat sex as just another topic of conversation, but one you're not that interested in. You only have to do this a couple of times before he realizes you're not into talking about it. So, just reply with a breezy 'Really? Fascinating!' then go on to chat about the merits of double-glazing, or your mother's bypass operation.

- Carry on as you were before. Don't feel guilty or hassled. If he is only dropping sex into the conversation, his lust is still at a manageable level.

- Yawn. This is a brilliant but under-used conversational tactic. Whenever something comes up that you don't want to talk about — from sex to exes to your waitress's low-cut blouse — just yawn so your jaw almost pops out of place and he'll change the subject. Promise.

First Month Panic

SURELY it's the right time now??

Why? He's proposed? That's fantastic! Congratulations! Let me see the ring ... oh, there doesn't seem to be one. So why on earth are you thinking about nobbing him? Listen, if you bonk him after just four weeks you are — in all likelihood — going to move straight into his 'Good For Now Girl' folder. He won't think you're a total goddess he must give up his bachelor freedom to possess. Yes, he might be happy and relieved, but doh, of course he will, he's just got laid. You want him to be crazy for you and that is not going to happen after a mere four weeks.

Tips:

- Have The Talk with him. If you haven't already, this is the right time to tell him that you aren't going to be having uncommitted sex any time soon. Say you are very tempted because you really like him, but you really aren't interested in having sex yet, until you can really see where the relationship is going. If he blurts out things like, 'But I'm mad about you! You know that. I'm not going anywhere,' say that that is wonderful to hear and it makes you very happy. Then carry on as you were. Men only get annoyed when they think you're either messing them around, or just not interested. If he keeps talking about it, say that 'to have sex now would just feel wrong to me'. He can't argue with your feelings.

- Keep seeing him on outdoor-type dates, and don't start having sleepovers yet.

- Listen and learn – this is a quote from a forty-year-old man: 'When I was dating, I put women into two categories: the first were "fun" girls with whom relationships would have a four-to-six-week shelf life, and the second were "potential partners" with whom I could see myself for more than six months.' Lots of men think like this, so the only way to find out for certain is to see if he continues to date you despite not getting anything. The pleasure of your company *will be enough* for any man who adores you.

Second Month Lust

This is hard.

Nope. Hard is waiting for the phone to ring when you suspect a bloke isn't that keen on you anymore. Hard is having to pluck up the courage to ask a man where he sees your relationship going. Hard is having the strength to leave a relationship when the man says he doesn't see himself getting married to you. Hard is being a single mother. Hard is having a termination. And hard is what his willy will continue to be every time he sees you before he's actually slept with you.

Tips:

- Throw some ice cubes down your bra, for goodness sake.
- Remind yourself that you are going to try this out properly and see what happens. Don't be impatient to call it all off – keep going. Take it one date at a time. This is exciting – you could end up married to a man who really worships you; he thinks you're special and different and better than any other woman he's ever met – or will meet in the future.
- Re-read the Success Stories chapter. That could be you!

Third Month Switch

He's starting to see more of his friends again now. We're falling into a routine. I think he's getting bored. A bit of a shag would really spice things up about now.

Be honest now: what would you be most excited to have on the next date with him – a frenzied bonk, or a heartfelt declaration of his feelings and love for you, plus the first hints that he is thinking about marriage?

If it's the bonk, are you going off him? Do you see him with you long term? Are you starting to discover he has annoying habits and/or hair on his back? In which case, don't you dare jump on him. Do you want to get more attached to him? Do you want to get so gaga you start lovingly plaiting those hairs? If you're not sure how you feel, don't do a thing. A couple more weeks will clarify your thoughts and then you can either continue to see him, or drop him, not your pants.

If it's the mushy stuff, then that's even *more* reason not to climb aboard the SS Titanic Todger. Finding it a struggle? Then read on:

Tip:

- Book a weekend away without him. Sometimes this is the only thing that can keep your mind on your own life.

Fourth Month Desire

Please, please let me shag him now. I've never waited this long, ever. It's getting so bad, I find myself gazing at his crotch on dates. I doodle penises in boring work meetings. I feel like a randy old lady – it's mad!

If you feel this excited, imagine how aroused he is getting. I know it's agony, but this is all GOOD. It shows that sex is becoming something very distracting and tempting and hot. You're probably surprised by your level of desire, because you've never denied yourself pleasure before. But lust *should* be at an almost unmanageable level before you satisfy it. This is how thrilling sex always *used* to be before we down-graded it to just another way to get your recommended daily thirty minutes of exercise.

Tips:

- Enjoy your lustiness. Don't feel you should be squashing it down like an irritating cough; instead, think of it as a sign that you are dating a man with whom you feel chemistry. This is good. The sex will be amazing when you finally have it.

- Keep an eye on the list of questions in Chapter Five. This will help you check how things are progressing. THIS IS NOT FOREVER.

- Use the last bits of your rationality to look at how he treats you and how you feel in his company. These sex-free months are not something to bravely endure before you get to the enjoyable parts of dating. These are important months when you check whether he's someone you should risk being bonded to.

Fifth Month Impatience

Okay, I'm furious with you. This is all just some pointless self-help book I wish I'd never read and it's bound to make this lovely man I'm dating finally snap with impatience and ditch me for being buttoned-up and barren and . . . oh, oh . . . I'm just HATING YOU right now.

Someone needs a shagging! But it's okay because you are only a handful of dates away from the most anticipated seeing-to you've ever had. Don't you see, you've *done* the hard bit. If this were an Everest expedition, you'd be camping on the side about fifty metres from the top. If this were childbirth (instead of its opposite), you'd be nine centimetres dilated and almost ready to push. If this were baking, you'd only have the birthday candles left to put on the top . . . You're almost there. Don't bail out now.

You don't appear 'buttoned-up and barren' when you don't have sex within a few months of meeting a new man. You look choosy. You look like sex is a big deal to you, which is *better* than looking like it's not.

I think this is something we all struggle with today. We long to be fiery fuck-goddesses who can jump men and dump them, leaving the poor, ravaged males to pine over us forever. We *want* to appear like sex isn't important to us, like we're all feisty and flighty . . . Like we're men, in other words. But we're not men, and so we can't ever pull off the act. We do get keen, we do get emotionally invested, and we do get upset if anything goes wrong.

Tips:

- Embrace your femininity. Don't feel you are denying yourself anything by not having sex. See it as a positive thing, a way to maintain your mystery, your lofty love goddess status. Remind yourself that anyone can have sex – it's a stronger, sassier woman who believes she is worth more than a no-strings rogering.

- Enjoy foreplay with your partner. After you've waited this long, of course you can enjoy all sorts of sexy stuff like massages, um . . . 'fondling', and the like. Be careful not to let it tempt you to go the whole way, but do start to enjoy more naughtiness if you think that will keep you going for the last few weeks.

Sixth Month Uncertainty

It's been six months now – hooray! – but I still can't say 'Yes' to all the questions in Chapter Five. What do I do?

Keep waiting. It's more important that you can see positive proof of his feelings for you, rather than the fact that he has stuck around for six months without getting lucky. By six months, most men will have demonstrated true affection, by fixing your stuff, calling you all the time and trying to make you a part of their life. If they haven't, it's a bit odd, like they're just treading water, not really keen to move things forwards.

Tip:

- Don't get worried or angry and start interrogating him about where he sees things going, but if he initiates a conversation about the future, you *can* reply honestly. After this long, you should be able to talk about things like marriage and children. If he seems perfectly happy where you are now, I would say that's worth thinking about. Most men know within a few months if you're The One, or just The Latest One.

Friends Without Benefits

Okay, I'm doing really well on not having sex with men that I fancy, but I am starting to fantasize about pulling a man in a club and boffing him.

I understand this urge. I call it 'Stranger Danger'. I've done this before, and it seemed like the best idea ever at the time. But looking back, the sex was never that good. One-night stands are usually a let down, because both of you pull your standard moves on each other, it's over quite quickly and halfway through there's always a moment when he does something that irritates you and you think, 'Gawd, why am I in bed with this twat?' From that moment on it's just a countdown to the point when you can acceptably call for a cab.

Tips:

- Channel all that sexual energy into work projects. Many artists used celibacy to inspire them and help them focus on great masterpieces. You could do something similar. Instead of trawling nightclubs looking for a penis, stay home and start writing a novel, think of new ways to decorate your home, take on extra work projects, sew a coat . . . these will have longer-lasting positive benefits on your life than bouncing up and down on someone's face.

- Channel more energy into looking for a partner, not a lover. Update your online dating advert (new photos will attract new men) or hold a party. Tell all your friends you're looking to meet someone new. If you meet Mr Right, you can have nookie whenever you like.

Should I bonk my ex-boyfriend? Surely he doesn't count?

See the above question and answer.

My male best friend is also single, and has jokingly suggested we have sex with each other while we wait for someone else to come along. You're going to tell me this is a bad idea, right?

You betcha! In fact I was just talking with a friend about this. She has a lovely male friend whom she's known for a couple of years. One night last month they got drunk together and he suggested they go to bed. So they did. It turned out he had a penis the size of a docker's arm, and the sex was wonderful. She was telling herself over and over, 'This means nothing, this means nothing' as she went to sleep. The next morning he woke up hung over and regretful. Before she had said a word, he began telling her how 'that didn't mean anything', he was 'not looking for a relationship', and that she wasn't his 'ideal body type'. Can you imagine? What annoyed her most – aside from being obliquely called fat – was the fact that Mr Cocky launched into all this before she had even had a chance to go clingy. He just assumed she would now be keen on him (which, to be fair, she was) and thought he'd better nip her interest in the bud. She ended up storming out, and spending the next couple of weeks avoiding him and crying on her bed. After they patched up their friendship, he was then back to telling her about his latest dating exploits.

This is obviously the worst-case scenario, but I haven't ever seen a just-good-friends shag turn into a thing of beauty. What usually happens is the woman gets keener, and the man remains maddeningly untouched. Avoid.

Tips:

- Laugh off your friend's suggestion. This will either be the end of it, or he will start to realize you mean more to him than he thought, and he'll begin to pursue you properly. If he does, you still have to wait six months before sex. Start the timer at the moment you have your first proper date, not from the moment you first met, years ago in infant school.

- Remind yourself that the less meaningless sex you have, the more energy you'll put into finding a partner.
- Ask your friend to think of male mates you might get on with. He'll be hopeless at this — men never set up their female friends with anyone worthwhile, it's almost as if they can't bear to help a man have sex with anyone they haven't first porked themselves — but you never know. If nothing else, he might be surprised at how jealous he feels by this, and be moved to start courting you. Or he'll set you up with someone fab. Good luck!

Sleepovers

What are your views on sleepovers? Are they allowed?

I think whether or not you allow sleepovers depends on two things: how much self-control you have, and how cherishing your boyfriend is. We can express this idea with formulae.

Determinedly Chaste Girl + Cherishing Boyfriend = No Sex.

Determinedly Chaste Girl + Uncherishing Boyfriend = No sex, possibly some arguments, definitely some male tutting.

Slightly Shaky Girl + Cherishing Boyfriend = Sex, but only after a long conversation about it, when he says things like, 'Are you sure? You know I can wait as long as you want me to' and she says things like, 'Oh, get your pants off before I change my mind.'

Slightly Shaky Girl + Uncherishing Boyfriend = Sex every possible way, followed by blissful sleep on the male side of the bed, anxious insomnia on the female side.

So it's up to you. It is possible to enjoy some chaste sleepovers with a lovely, innocent Fifties feel to them, with you wearing the pyjama top and him wearing the bottoms, but I wouldn't risk it if you feel even vaguely doubtful you can hold out. What can happen is that he accepts there will be no sex and starts to fall asleep. You then lie there feeling annoyed and contrary, and start dreaming up reasons why you should jump on him. And then jump on him. And then wake up the next day and think 'Arse'.

Tips:

- Wear lots of clothes. Several bras, a week's worth of pants, tights *and* socks. Anything complicated with locks is good.

- Only allow sleepovers the night before a busy day. Even if you get through the night sex-free, waking up next to your Dream Man can destroy the last of your self-control. Men are also more randy in the morning, so don't expect him to be able to hold back like a monk when he wakes up. Have a reason to be up and out of that bed before anything can arise.

- Don't have a sleepover during the first three months of dating him. Apart from the risk of nookie, sleepovers are also a bit too intense. They're intimate and revealing. He gets to see you with bed-hair, he gets to hear your snoring. There's no mystery with a sleep-over date.

- Don't get into the habit of sleepovers. Just because you had one last Saturday doesn't mean you must have one next Saturday. Don't buy him a toothbrush or razor to keep at your place, and likewise don't fill his flat with spare hairdryers and eye make-up remover pads.

Holidays

My boyfriend has asked me to go away for the weekend with him. Am I allowed to bonk him, please?

No. Unless you can answer 'Yes' to all the questions in Chapter Five, I can't give you a Weekend Nookie Pass, I'm afraid. It's a lovely sign that your boyfriend wants to take you away for the weekend, but it doesn't negate all the other advice in the book. I will now give you five minutes to stomp around grumpily, then please read the following tips:

Tips:

- Don't feel you have to warn him straight out that sex won't be on the weekend itinerary. If you did, I think it would make you sound guilty, especially if he is paying for the trip. (Which he should be, of course.) Really he shouldn't *expect* anything to change just because you're both in a different location, although he might hope that it will.

- If you feel it might turn into a wrestling match in the hotel room, you could obliquely state your opinion. Something like 'I'd feel more comfortable if we had separate rooms, is that possible?' is good. Or just check that he's booked a room with twin beds.

- Don't let yourself be pressured into bonking him just to somehow repay him for the trip. Nice men wouldn't let you feel bad, of course, but selfish men can manipulate you into bed any way possible. If he kicks up a fuss, ask reception for a separate room and then ditch him the minute you get home.

- If you're worried you'll never resist Hotel Sex, try to plan the trip for a weekend when you have your period. This is extreme, but effective.

My boyfriend has invited me on holiday. I'd love to go, but surely a sex-free holiday will be a nightmare?

If it's a holiday with lots of other people, it'll be fine. But a holiday with just the two of you could be odd without naughtiness. Unless the vacation will correspond with your six-month anniversary, and you can answer 'Yes' to the questions in Chapter Five, I'd politely refuse the trip. Everything feels different on holiday – all your best don't-get-laid plans could easily go out of the window.

Tips:

- Group holidays with lots of people are much easier to handle. See if you can share a room with another girl. No swapping rooms again when you're there!
- If it's within the first three months of dating, holidays of any kind are usually a bad idea if you want to keep any sort of mystery.

Afterword

I honestly believe that all women's relationships will be transformed by the simple method of withholding sex until commitment. I've tried to keep this book light-hearted as the last thing you want is to give up sex *and* fun simultaneously. But there is a serious message here. Love is much, much easier, more successful and more fulfilling when you keep a part of yourself back. Yes, I mean *that* part, your lady-part. But I also mean a small part of yourself that remains untouched by the man in your life.

We are more emotionally vulnerable than men, who have always been able to compartmentalize their interests. As Byron said, 'Love is to men a thing apart, 'tis woman's whole existence.' When you give sex away as if it means very little, you are making yourself more vulnerable to being hurt or becoming too involved. Far wiser to be a lofty love goddess, who remains objective about what is such a huge part of our lives.

Don't feel tempted to try and be cold and unemotional about love and sex. Don't feel you can out-bloke a man, and have sex as lightly as he can. It's too dangerous. You give away too much of yourself.

Instead, begin treasuring your vulnerability and protecting it. When you meet Mr Right, don't be afraid to end dates with just a kiss. Be sassy. Think of yourself as different and special. Know that you are worthy of being Mrs Right. Because you are. And you will be.

Further Nagging...
Sorry, Reading

I'm not the only woman who wants to make sure that you never have sex again. There's a small pack of us. We roam the world like dried-up nuns, spreading the gospel on keeping your legs crossed. If you'd like to read more, these are (in my opinion) the best books on the subject.

A Return to Modesty, by Wendy Shalit (Pocketbooks, January 2000).

If It's Love You're After, Why Settle for (Just) Sex?, by Laurie Langford (Prima Publishing US, May 1996).

Getting To I Do, by Dr Patricia Allen (Avon Books, February 1995). (Includes a really good chapter on oxytocin and bonding.)

Why Men Love Bitches, by Sherrie Argov (Adams Media Corporation, October 2002). (Explains very well the idea of giving up your 'candy store' one 'jujube at a time'.)

The Technique of the Love Affair, by Doris Langley Moore, has now been reprinted with notes and additions by Norrie Epstein (Books Sales, 2002). (This is the classic relationship book which I mentioned in the first chapter. I urge you to buy a copy.)

More tips, advice and last-minute support are available at www.nottonightmrright.com

Acknowledgements

Many people helped bring this book to life, but I feel special thanks must be given for the outstanding contributions made by the following females: Kate Adams, Lizzy Kremer, Katie Szita, Miranda Higham, Fiona Brown, Elisabeth Merriman, Katie Sheppard and my brilliant, brilliant Mum, Anne Taylor – thank you.

Live more

FREE trial at
match.com !*

Looking for love?

We are offering every reader a FREE 7 day trial* with the world's number one internet dating website **match**.com. Unlimited access to everything on the **match**.com site within this time period means that you can communicate with potential partners safely and privately. You will be able to search the site, create a profile, find your matches and most importantly, set up dates! This will be made easy by sending and receiving emails as much as you like during the 7 days – **FOR FREE!**

 Claiming your free trial couldn't be easier – simply visit **www.match.com/mrright** and click on the subscribe button. You will be asked to fill in your personal details and provide credit card information.

Kate Taylor herself met her husband on **match**.com in 2000, so who knows what might happen! She is one of 400,000 people a year who find the relationship they are searching for on the number one site for love.

ENJOY YOUR FREE TRIAL!